CITIZENSHIP AND THE CONSTITUTION

TO ESTABLISH

JUSTICE

Patricia McKissack and Arlene Zarembka

Alfred A. Knopf
NEW YORK

All quotations from court decisions and the Constitution in this book use the original words, punctuation, and spelling. Due to changes in American English usage over the past two hundred years, the way these documents were written may not conform to modern American English usage.

To my grandsons, with the hope that they will always live in freedom
—P.McK.

To my mother, Helen Jane Zarembka, and to the memory of my father, Richard Zarembka,
both of whom instilled in me a commitment to justice and equality,
and to those who have sought to make the constitutional guarantees of
equality and liberty a reality for all who live in the United States
—A.Z.

THIS IS A BORZOI BOOK PUBLISHED BY ALFRED A. KNOPF
Copyright © 2004 by Patricia McKissack and Arlene Zarembka
Cover flag photo copyright © Corbis
(top right inset on cover) Photo copyright © Bettmann/Corbis
(middle left inset on cover) Photo copyright © Ilka Hartmann, "We will not give up"
(Oohosis, a Cree from Canada, after the removal from Alcatraz Island on June 11, 1971)
(middle right inset on cover) Photo copyright © Schulke/Corbis
(bottom left inset on cover) Photo copyright © National Archives and Records Administration
All rights reserved under International and Pan-American Copyright Conventions. Published in the United States by Alfred A. Knopf, an imprint of Random House Children's Books, a division of Random House, Inc., New York, and simultaneously in Canada by Random House of Canada Limited, Toronto.
Distributed by Random House, Inc., New York.

KNOPF, BORZOI BOOKS, and the colophon are registered trademarks of Random House, Inc.

www.randomhouse.com/teens

Library of Congress Cataloging-in-Publication Data
McKissack, Pat, 1944–
To establish justice : citizenship and the Constitution / Patricia McKissack, Arlene Zarembka. — 1st ed.
p. cm.
"Published simultaneously in Canada by Random House of Canada Limited, Toronto"—T.p. verso.
ISBN 0-679-89308-3 (trade) — ISBN 0-679-99308-8 (lib. bdg.)
1. Discrimination—Law and legislation—United States. [1. Discrimination—Law and legislation.]
I. Zarembka, Arlene. II. Title.
KF4755.Z9M388 2004
342.7308'7—dc22
2003027929

Printed in the United States of America
September 2004
10 9 8 7 6 5 4 3 2 1
First Edition

CONTENTS

WE THE PEOPLE OF THE UNITED STATES,
IN ORDER TO FORM A MORE PERFECT
UNION, ESTABLISH JUSTICE, INSURE
DOMESTIC TRANQUILITY, PROVIDE FOR
THE COMMON DEFENSE, PROMOTE
THE GENERAL WELFARE, AND SECURE THE
BLESSINGS OF LIBERTY TO OURSELVES AND
OUR POSTERITY, DO ORDAIN AND ESTABLISH
THIS CONSTITUTION FOR THE UNITED
STATES OF AMERICA.

—U.S. CONSTITUTION, PREAMBLE

INTRODUCTION

Three questions have been at the heart of the conflict over justice and equality for over two hundred years:

- Who is a citizen?

- Should all citizens of the United States have equal rights?

- Who ensures that the rights of citizens are protected?

The nation and the courts have addressed these questions time and again in determining the status and rights of Native Americans, African Americans, immigrants, women, disabled people, students, and gay men and lesbians. This book is the story of the struggle by members of these groups for justice and the interpretation of their rights as guaranteed by the U.S. Constitution.

The answers to the above citizenship questions have changed as society's attitudes and opinions have evolved. Although the judges who interpret the Constitution are supposed to be impartial, they are human beings and are subject to their own biases and those imposed on them by their times. A judge who dares to go against popular opinion and the political climate often finds himself or herself ridiculed or a lone dissenter. In the final analysis, however, such a judge is often vindicated.

The Constitution is a document that makes change possible without the civil strife usually associated with growth and development.

The Declaration of Independence declared that "all men are created equal, that they are endowed by their Creator with certain unalienable Rights." Nevertheless, the original Constitution didn't grant equal rights. In fact, it specifically allowed slavery and failed to grant voting rights to all citizens.

But after the Civil War, the Constitution was amended to grant African Americans citizenship. Native Americans generally didn't become citizens until the late nineteenth and early twentieth centuries. The Fifteenth Amendment gave black men the right to vote, but it took two other amendments to grant women and eighteen-year-olds suffrage. Arguments still continue over which immigrants should be allowed to become citizens.

Not until 1868 did the Constitution provide any equal protection guarantees. It was the Fourteenth Amendment that, among other things, finally prohibited states from denying equal protection of the laws to any person. Nevertheless, African Americans and other ethnic minorities endured decades of state-enforced segregation, and the Supreme Court gave its blessing to these denials of equal rights.

Some of the answers to the citizenship questions seem to be contained in the Constitution and its amendments. But the Constitution is subject to interpretation. As society and the justices on the Supreme Court have changed, the Court's interpretations of the Constitution have changed. Justice and equality do not have fixed meanings; instead, their definitions change over time.

The conflict over extending equal rights guarantees, and even the meaning of the term, continues to this day. The courts are repeatedly asked to make decisions about what equal rights are and who is entitled to these guaranteed protections. During your lifetime, and the lifetimes of the generations to come, the three citizenship questions will be debated, and the answers will keep changing.

This book is an introduction to the struggle for equal rights and how courts have addressed the three questions regarding the rights of minority groups and women.

Ordinary people have had a powerful influence on the meaning of justice and on how the Constitution has been interpreted. They still do. This, then, is the story of ordinary Americans—like you—who have fought for the rights to be free and to be treated equally and respectfully under the law. As you will learn, the road to justice is not straight; it has many twists and turns, hills and valleys. It is certain there will continue to be many forks in the road to justice. Meanwhile, let us show you how far our nation has come in the last two hundred years.

"To Say What the Law Is . . .": Who Defines the Rights of Citizens?

The Constitution Says . . .
"The judicial Power of the United States shall be vested in one supreme Court. . . ."
—U.S. Constitution, Article III, Section 1

Two of the founding fathers had this to say about the U.S. Constitution: George Washington called the document the "precious depository of American happiness." Thomas Jefferson praised it another way: "The Constitution is the ark of our safety . . . it belongs to the living and not the dead." Because the framers recognized this, the Constitution has stood the test of time. Illustration of the Constitutional Convention of 1787 from *A History of the United States of America* (1823).

The U.S. Constitution is the world's oldest written constitution. It has lasted so long because of its flexibility and because of the checks and balances provided by its writers, called the framers.

Over the long, hot summer of 1787, the delegates to the Constitutional Convention in Philadelphia debated behind closed doors how the new nation should be governed. In the end, the delegates agreed upon a federal system—the existing Articles of Confederation, in which the national government was relatively weak and the state governments relatively strong. The new Constitution strengthened the powers of the central (federal) government and limited some of the powers of state governments.

By June 21, 1788, after considerable debate over the pros and cons of the document, two-thirds of the states had ratified the Constitution, and it went into effect the following March.

The framers of the Constitution feared that a single federal power would become corrupt and oppressive, so they established three independent governing branches—the executive branch, headed by the president; the legislative branch, headed by Congress; and the judicial branch, headed by the Supreme Court. To keep any person, group, or governmental branch from grasping unlimited power, the framers established a series of checks and balances to control and equalize the branches.

Here's an example of how it works. Congress has the authority to pass a bill, which the president can veto or sign into law. Congress can override a veto by a two-thirds majority, making the bill a law whether the president approves it or not. However, if the Supreme Court declares it *unconstitutional*, the law is not valid. Although the president can't make a law, he or she can issue an executive order, which doesn't have to be approved by Congress. But if the order is challenged, the Supreme Court can rule whether the action is in keeping with U.S. law or the Constitution.

Abraham Lincoln's Emancipation Proclamation is a good example of how an executive order can be used by a president. Lincoln didn't have the constitutional authority to abolish slavery. However, he used his executive power as commander in chief of the Union Army to free slaves as a military strategy. By freeing the slaves, Lincoln disrupted the Confederate Army, which used slave labor to support the South's rebellion. Later, the Thirteenth Amendment to the Constitution abolished

One famous example of the Supreme Court reversing a former decision is the 1896 *Plessy v. Ferguson* case. In 1896, the High Court ruled that racially separate public accommodations and facilities weren't necessarily unconstitutional if they were "separate but equal." That ruling ushered in a half century of segregation and discrimination.

In 1954, almost sixty years later, a Supreme Court with different members looked at the same Constitution and interpreted it differently. In *Brown v. Board of Education of Topeka, Kansas*, the High Court ruled that "separate" was "inherently unequal" and therefore unconstitutional, in effect overturning the *Plessy* decision.

slavery in the United States.

The checks and balances are reflected in the way Supreme Court justices (and other federal court judges) are chosen. The president (executive branch) nominates them, but they must be confirmed by a majority vote of the Senate (legislative branch).

Federal judges and Supreme Court justices serve for life. However, they can resign or be removed by impeachment for misconduct or failure to perform their duties. The framers hoped that without the worry of reelection, justices could make decisions that weren't swayed by public opinion or the politics of the day. But Supreme Court decisions are a matter of interpretation, and personal, political, and cultural biases have, in fact, swayed opinions.

The framers were wise enough to realize that they had not crafted a perfect document and therefore made provisions for it to be changed. The Supreme Court has the final word regarding constitutional matters. Neither Congress nor the president can change a court decision that interprets

The U.S. Constitution (drafted in 1787, ratified in 1788, and put into effect 1789)

the Constitution. Such a decision can be changed only by the Supreme Court itself or by a constitutional amendment.

During the ratification debates of 1787, one of the primary concerns was that the Constitution didn't protect the individual rights of ordinary citizens. The original Constitution didn't contain a statement, such as the one found in the Declaration of Independence, that "all men are created equal." In fact, the Constitution ratified in 1788 provided for almost no individual rights, concentrating instead on protecting *property rights*.

But feelings about individual rights were very strong. The first Congress, which met in 1789, addressed this concern by proposing twelve amendments to the Constitution. Ten of the amendments, known as the Bill of Rights, were ratified by the states and became part of the Constitution in 1791.

The Bill of Rights guaranteed important liberties, such as free speech, freedom of religion, and the rights of those accused of crimes. But contrary to popular misconception, it did not ensure equal rights. It did not prohibit slavery; it did not grant voting rights; it did not prevent race or sex discrimination. Equal rights guarantees didn't appear in the Constitution until after the Civil War.

When the Constitution was ratified, it left open the question of citizenship: Who is or can become a citizen of the United States? Should Native Americans be considered citizens? And what are the rights and protections of all citizens? These primary questions have been at the core of the struggle for justice and equality.

The Constitution used the word "citizen" (or "citizenship") in several places but left defining it up to Congress and the states. At the time of the Constitution's adoption, women, most free blacks, and white men without property were disenfranchised, which means they were not allowed to vote. Given the social climate of the day, the idea of granting suffrage (the right to vote) to women wasn't even considered.

Obviously the term "citizen" meant something different then than it does today. In the eighteenth century, most women and poor white men didn't own land, but they didn't question the authority of the framers, who were for the most part wealthy white men. None of the delegates at the Constitutional Convention were elected by popular vote, and two-thirds were below age fifty. None were women. None were African Americans, Native Americans, or other people of color. None were of the Jewish, Muslim, or Hindu faiths. None were ordinary seamen, farmers, craftsmen, or laborers. Forty-seven of the fifty-five delegates were land speculators,

Engraving of a slave auction in Virginia (1861)

The Constitution's Protection of Slavery

• The Fugitive Slave Clause (Article IV, Section 2, Clause 3) required that any slave or indentured servant who escaped into another state had to be returned to his or her master.

• It prohibited Congress from interfering with the slave trade until the year 1808 (Article I, Section 9, Clause 1 and Article V).

• It apportioned representatives in Congress according to the free population of each state (including indentured servants, but excluding most Indians), plus "three fifths of all other persons" (Article I, Section 2, Clause 3). Who were "all other persons"? The slaves. By counting three-fifths of the slaves in determining the number of representatives that each state had in Congress, the South got more representatives (and therefore more power) in the House of Representatives and in the electoral college, which selected the president, than if slaves had not been counted.

• Slaveholders could be taxed only on three-fifths of their slaves (Article I, Section 9, Clause 4 and Article I, Section 2, Clause 3). This gave Southerners an incentive to buy slaves rather than other types of property, because their "property tax" on slaves was lower than their tax on other property.

• The Senate had two senators from each state. Two-thirds of the Senate had to agree to any constitutional amendment proposed by Congress. Because Southern senators constituted over one-third of the Senate, no constitutional amendment that threatened the institution of slavery could be approved.

• Finally, the Constitution limited the tax on slaves from overseas to ten dollars and prohibited any taxes on exports, meaning that slave-labor products could not be taxed (Article I, Section 9, Clause 1 and Clause 5).

Nineteenth-century engraving of George Washington

lenders, or merchants. Fifteen of the delegates owned slaves, including George Washington, who chaired the convention. Although they had no vote, women, landless white men, and three-fifths of all slaves were counted in determining the total number of representatives each state would have.

The Constitution also safeguarded the rights of slaveholders. Its protection of slavery was disguised in several sections and clauses without ever using the words "slave" or "slavery." Only a careful person reading between the lines would learn that slaves were excluded from those protections guaranteed by the government. Slavery would be an issue the Supreme Court would have to contend with as the nation developed.

Ratification of the Constitution did not assure the success of the new government.

Portrait of Thomas Jefferson by Charles Balthazar Julien Fevret de Saint-Mémin (1805)

6 George Washington, the first elected president; the men who served in his cabinet; and the members of the first Congress had actively supported the Constitution. They were Federalists. Those who opposed the Constitution were anti-Federalists.

Alexander Hamilton, John Adams, and John Marshall led the Federalists. Thomas Jefferson led the anti-Federalists. Hamilton and Jefferson were equally matched adversaries, very much like two titans poised to fight a battle of ideas. Knowing what these two men were at odds about is essential to understanding the early days of the Republic and the formation of partisan politics in the United States. The Federalists believed that people needed to be governed, and that the way to build America was by expanding its commerce and manufacturing. Anti-Federalists were

leery of a strong federal court system because they feared it would lead to tyranny. Those who agreed with Hamilton's ideas formed the Federalist Party. Those who agreed with Jefferson formed the Democratic-Republican Party, later called the Republican Party.

Alexander Hamilton, one of the framers, wrote in *The Federalist Papers:* "Laws are a dead letter without courts to expound and define their true meaning and operation." For that purpose, Congress passed the Judiciary Act of 1789, which established thirteen district courts and three circuit courts of appeal. (Today there are ninety-four dis-

Portrait of Alexander Hamilton by William Rollinson (1800)

trict courts and thirteen circuit courts of appeal.) It granted to the Supreme Court the power to review all federal suits as well as all state-court decisions that involve federal issues.

John Jay, the first person to hold the office of chief justice of the Supreme Court, was appointed in 1789 and served until 1795. The chief justice presides over the Supreme Court and the other justices. Although the chief justice has only one vote, as the other justices do, he or she can set the agenda for the court. And if the chief justice votes with the majority in a case, he or she can decide which justice will write the majority opinion.

During the first session of the Supreme Court in 1790, Jay and his fellow justices wore black and red robes and avoided the powdered wigs that Jefferson said made English judges look like "rats peering through bunches of hemp."

In the early days, the justices met in makeshift quarters because there was no Supreme Court building. Neither the justices nor the High Court had much influence or prestige.

Gradually, however, the Supreme Court became the most powerful court within the judicial branch of the federal government, largely because of John Marshall.

John Marshall was appointed as chief justice in 1801 and served for thirty-four years. Under Marshall's leadership the High Court claimed the authority to interpret the meaning of the Constitution, overturn decisions made by lower courts, and decide whether federal, state, or local laws and actions are constitutional. As a Fed-

Portrait of Chief Justice John Jay by Joseph Wright (1888)

7

eralist justice, Marshall did more to shape the role of the Supreme Court than anyone before him.

One of the most important decisions Chief Justice Marshall made was in the 1803 *Marbury v. Madison* case. He established the principle that the Constitution is binding on all branches of government as the final law of the land. He also ruled that federal judges can declare void those laws that they decide violate the Constitution. He wrote: "It is emphatically the province and duty of the judicial department to say what the law is."

Chief Justice Marshall also established two other key legal principles. In 1819, he ruled that the Constitution gives Congress the implied power to pass any laws that are helpful in carrying out its responsibilities. "Let the end be legitimate," Marshall wrote, "let it be within the scope of the constitution, and all means which are appropriate, which are plainly adapted to that end, which are not prohibited, but consistent with the letter and spirit of the constitution, are constitutional."

In 1824, he ruled that the federal government had the right to regulate interstate commerce and could overrule state actions that were inconsistent with federal authority. The 1824 decision angered the anti-Federalists, who wanted the states to have more power and the federal government to have less. One hundred forty years later, Chief Justice Marshall's decision allowed the Supreme Court to rule that the 1964 Civil Rights Act was constitutional.

States rights advocates such as Thomas Jefferson, who led the Republicans, strongly opposed the Marshall court's decisions. They argued that Congress could only pass those laws that were *indispensable* to carrying out the powers granted to Congress by the Constitution. Nevertheless, Jefferson was not able to diminish Federalist domination of the courts.

By 1811, most of the Supreme Court justices had been appointed by Republican presidents who opposed Federalism. Even so, these justices agreed, in most cases, with Marshall's expansive Federalist interpretation of the Constitution. The Federalist vision of a strong national government was firmly established in American constitutional law well before the end of Marshall's service on the Supreme Court in 1835.

"A Domestic Dependent Nation": Can Citizens Take the Land of Noncitizens?

The Constitution Says . . .

"The judicial Power shall extend to . . . Controversies . . . between a State . . . and foreign States, Citizens or Subjects."
—U.S. Constitution, Article III, Section 2, Clause 1

"This Constitution, and the Laws of the United States which shall be made in Pursuance thereof; and all Treaties made . . . under the Authority of the United States, shall be the supreme Law of the Land. . . ."
—U.S. Constitution, Article VI, Clause 2

Two Seminole chiefs captured by Andrew Jackson's forces (1818)

Land.

The Indians had it. The United States wanted it.

Conflict was inevitable.

European settlers arrived in the Western Hemisphere with the belief that land was a primary source of individual wealth and power. White men who held large estates were usually well-respected leaders in the community. They were politically powerful and able to vote. Land was also a primary means of exchange. By buying and selling it, and using the natural resources on it to produce marketable products such as food, cotton, and tobacco, individuals amassed great fortunes in the New World.

Native Americans had a different mindset. They didn't believe land should be— or even could be—individually owned, bought, or sold. They considered themselves the caretakers of the land, woods, mountains, valleys, rivers, and lakes, as well as all the creatures that roamed freely in them. A fence was unnecessary and so was a deed. And they used only the resources needed to sustain life.

From the moment the two peoples came into contact with each other, there was conflict over these opposing ideas about land use and ownership. To most nineteenth-century whites, Native Americans were savages. They were not considered "civilized" until they accepted Christianity, settled down as farmers, learned household tasks, used money, and abandoned their own language in favor of English. The truest test of civilized groups was their adoption of individual property rights—a concept most native people totally rejected. Even so, the Cherokee, Chickasaw, Choctaw, Seminole, and Creek nations adopted many white customs. White society called them the Five Civilized Tribes, but the treatment they experienced was most uncivilized.

As whites became more powerful and their numbers increased, they insisted on more land. Lands outside the legal boundaries of a state, but owned by the United

President Jefferson repeatedly told Indian tribes that the United States was interested in buying their lands but assured them he would never pressure them to sell. Yet Jefferson pursued policies designed to result in the Indians' losing their lands. These included establishing government trading posts on Native American territory so that tribes would run up debts buying goods; their growing indebtedness would then compel them to sell their land to the government. He also encouraged Indians to give up hunting, become "civilized," and settle down on individual plots as farmers. Why? Because it would be easier to get individual Indians to sell their land than it would whole tribes.

Moreover, in 1802, Jefferson's administration approved an agreement with the state of Georgia that eventually resulted in the removal of all Cherokees from the state. In return for Georgia giving up lands that it claimed west of its boundaries at that time, the U.S. government pledged to eliminate all Indian claims to land within state boundaries "as early as the same can be peacably obtained, upon reasonable terms." It also paid Georgia $1.25 million (about $21 million today).

The Louisiana Purchase of 1803 provided the perfect "solution" by opening up a huge area of land west of the Mississippi River that could be used for resettlement of Indians who lived east of the great river. Jefferson argued that Indians either had to become "civilized" or else be moved west of the Mississippi.

States and subject to federal laws and protections, were called territories.

The problem was that members of the Five Civilized Tribes already occupied some of this land.

The Indians tried to get along with whites who moved into these areas. Those who weren't already farmers began farming and built permanent homes. Some practiced Christianity. Others adopted a written language and spoke English.

Still, many whites insisted that no Indian should be allowed to live east of the Mississippi River. Over many years, they pushed for legislation that finally resulted in an order for all the eastern tribes to move to the Oklahoma Territory. The Cherokee people led the fight against this removal in court. This is their story.

As the fledgling United States began to grow and prosper, hunters, trappers, and traders pushed westward into parts of the country protected by treaties. These adventurers returned to New York and other large eastern cities with wild and wonderful stories about land that was so abundant with game a person didn't need to worry about hunting or fishing. Supper jumped into the frying pan. And the land was reported to be so fertile a person needed only to mash a seed in the ground and a plant would sprout. Stories such as these— exaggerated though they were—inspired settlers to seek their fortunes in the western frontier. Whites pushed their state and federal leaders to open up Native American land for settlement. The mood of the nation grew decisively anti-Indian.

As a result of treaties, the Cherokees

An important 1823 Supreme Court decision, *Johnson v. McIntosh*, written by Chief Justice Marshall, aided the removal of Indians. Chief Justice Marshall ruled that the Indians didn't own their land. He held that European explorers had obtained title to the land in the New World on behalf of European nations simply by being the first *whites* to discover the land. The United States then obtained title to the land by treaties with European countries and could take lands occupied by Indians at any time by purchase or conquest.

ended up ceding (surrendering) most of their land to the federal government. In spite of the laws and treaties protecting remaining Indian land, settlers blatantly violated the borders and pushed the government to make even more Indian territory available for purchase. The government, in turn, sold it to land speculators, who resold it to individuals at a tremendous profit.

By the 1820s, whites in Georgia insisted that the Indians be removed from their state. This would make the Cherokees' rich lands, good streams, and timber available to white settlers and would allow the expansion of cotton production, which was the main crop of Southern plantations. A federal Indian agent proposed that the Cherokees be allotted 640 acres per family, with the rest sold to whites. Georgia whites rejected the proposal. They didn't want the Cherokees to have any land at all. (The Cherokees also rejected the plan because they would have to give up the majority of their domain.)

Presidential candidate Andrew Jackson made Indian removal one of his campaign themes in 1827. He had made a name for himself as the hero of the War of 1812 and during the Seminole Wars in Florida.

Emboldened by Jackson's election as president, Georgia adopted a law annexing territory occupied by the Cherokees and extending Georgia law over those lands. During the next two years, Georgia passed statutes abolishing Cherokee law and stating that an agreement between a Cherokee and a white man was unenforceable unless two whites testified to the agreement. At the same time, the statute denied Cherokees the right to testify against any white person in a Georgia court. But the most devastating law was one allowing Cherokee lands without buildings to be divided up and sold by lottery to whites.

The actions of the Georgia legislature and governor between 1828 and 1830 encouraged whites to flood onto Cherokee land. They seized Cherokee farms, livestock, and improvements and drove the Cherokees into the woods. The state militia attacked Indians who hunted within state lines. Since Georgia law prohibited Indians from testifying against a white person, the Cherokees could not look to the Georgia courts to help them.

As he had promised, President Andrew Jackson made Indian removal a top priority of his administration. The Indian Removal Act, passed by Congress in May 1830 after a bitter debate, authorized the president to try to move the Indians west of the Mississippi River, although all existing treaties with Indian tribes were not to be violated. It was a total betrayal of trust between the Indians and the government.

President Jackson's administration used coercion to get Indians to sign new treaties that agreed to removal. President Jackson told the Indians in Georgia that they remained there at their own risk. He also told Congress that he wouldn't enforce the Indians' rights if that conflicted with Georgia's wishes.

With the state of Georgia and the executive branch of the U.S. government arrayed against them, the Cherokees sought protection from the Supreme Court. Shortly after the Indian Removal Act passed, the Cherokee Nation filed a lawsuit entitled *The Cherokee Nation v. The State of Georgia,* asking the Court to prohibit Georgia from enforcing its laws against the Cherokees.

The Supreme Court threw out the Cherokee Nation's case against Georgia in a four-to-two decision. It also did not rule whether Georgia's actions were illegal under federal law and treaties with the Cherokees. Although sympathetic to the Cherokees' claim, Chief Justice Marshall, who wrote the majority opinion, focused his attention on whether the Cherokee Nation had any right to file a lawsuit in federal courts.

The Constitution states in Article III, Section 2 that federal courts can hear cases involving treaties or disputes between a state and a foreign government. Even though Chief Justice Marshall agreed that the federal government had "plainly recognize[d] the Cherokee Nation as a State" with which the federal government had made treaties, he ruled that the Cherokee Nation was not a *foreign* state.

Instead, Chief Justice Marshall called the Cherokee people a "domestic dependent nation." He wrote:

> They occupy a territory to which we assert a title independent of their will. . . . Meanwhile they are in a state of pupilage. Their relation to the United States resembles that of a ward to his guardian.

Because he concluded that the Cherokee Nation was not a foreign state, he ruled that it had no right to sue in the courts of the United States.

Not giving up the legal fight, the Cherokees found another avenue to get the Supreme Court to hear their claims that Georgia's anti-Cherokee laws violated federal laws and treaties. Among the laws that Georgia had passed in 1830 was one that prohibited whites from living on Indian lands unless they had a license from the state and took an oath to support the constitution and laws of Georgia. The purpose of this law was to drive whites sympathetic to the Indians off Indian land, as the *Worcester v. The State of Georgia* case illustrates.

Reverend Samuel A. Worcester was a white postmaster and missionary who had been working with the Cherokees for years. He refused to get a state license or give an oath of allegiance as demanded by law. The state of Georgia ordered Reverend Worcester to leave Georgia. When he refused, he was convicted of violating the 1830 license and oath-of-allegiance law and sentenced to four years of hard labor.

Reverend Worcester appealed to the Supreme Court. The same attorneys who had represented the Cherokees in the *Cherokee Nation v. The State of Georgia* represented Reverend Worcester. Chief Justice Marshall again wrote the opinion of the Court. But this time the Court ruled in favor of the Cherokee Nation in a five-to-one decision.

Chief Justice Marshall ruled that the state of Georgia had no authority to pass laws concerning Indian nations (including the Cherokee Nation) because only the *federal* government could make treaties and regulate trade with the Indians. Therefore, Georgia had no right to make any laws pertaining to Cherokee Territory, nor to invade Cherokee land, and Reverend Worcester's conviction under Georgia's laws was void.

Although the *Worcester* decision was a great legal victory for the Cherokee people, it became a meaningless piece of paper. Both the state of Georgia and President Jackson ignored the decision. Georgia refused to release Reverend Worcester from jail until many months later. President Jackson was reported to have said, "John Marshall has made his decision; now let him enforce it." He took no steps to protect the Cherokees in Georgia. Until the end of his term, President Jackson maintained a hard-line position that the only "solution" to the Cherokees' conflict with Georgia was for them to agree to removal west of the Mississippi River. In the end, the Cherokees were forced to move to Indian Territory (now Oklahoma), an eight-hundred-mile trek along what came to be called the Trail of Tears.

Lithograph of Cherokee Chief John Ross (1843)

removal. (The Georgia Guard arrested Chief John Ross before the meeting at which the treaty would be discussed, to prevent him from attending.) Although almost 16,000 Cherokees signed a petition *opposing* the treaty, out of a total eastern Cherokee population of about 16,500 (not counting almost 1,600 slaves and 200 whites and free blacks who were married to Cherokees), the U.S. Senate ratified the treaty by one vote.

General Winfield Scott was placed in charge of the forced removal. He ordered stockades built for holding the Cherokees as prisoners and began forcible removal in May 1838. He sent troops to bring in all Cherokee families, which the soldiers did by surrounding the houses without warning at mealtimes. The Cherokees were given only a short time to gather their belongings before they were forced to leave their homes. They often were driven out at the point of bayonets. Frequently whites set the Cherokee houses on fire as soon as the troops had left with the families, then

Although Cherokee leaders such as Chief John Ross strenuously resisted removal, the U.S. government finally was able to find a few Cherokees in 1835 who were willing to sign a treaty agreeing to

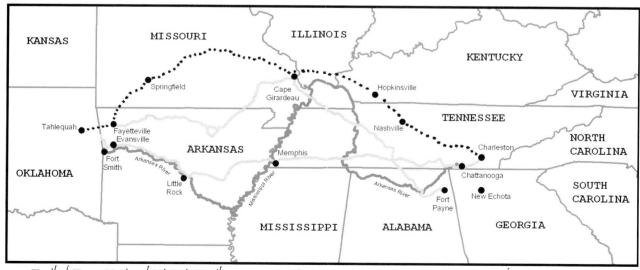

Trail of Tears National Historic Trail: ••••••• Land Route ⸻ Water Route ⸻ Other Major Routes

took their remaining property and livestock and looted their graves for silver.

During their trek westward, many Cherokees were forced to abandon much of the property they had brought with them, in order to lighten the load—utensils, bedding, looms, ovens, spinning wheels, farm implements, hoes, plows. Often they had to travel on foot, some barefoot, even in winter weather. Many died of cholera. When the terrible ordeal was over, about one-fourth of the eastern Cherokee Nation had died on the Trail of Tears.

Four other southeastern tribes also were expelled from their lands in the 1830s—the death toll was staggering. The Choctaws lost 4,000 of 14,000 members during their expulsion from Mississippi to Oklahoma in 1831 and 1832. The Creeks lost one-third of their tribe of 15,000 during removal. The Seminoles were deported from Florida as military prisoners in 1838.

The Cherokees' travails didn't end with their removal. The federal government, with the approval of the Supreme Court, continued to undermine the Cherokee Nation and the sovereignty rights of all Indian tribes and nations.

For example, an 1866 treaty with the Cherokee Nation provided that Cherokees could sell any product of their farms and other merchandise within Cherokee territory without having to pay U.S. taxes. Still, in 1868, the U.S. Revenue Act imposed federal taxes on the sale of tobacco and liquor, including on Cherokee land. Despite the

Painting of the Trail of Tears by Robert Lindneux (twentieth century)

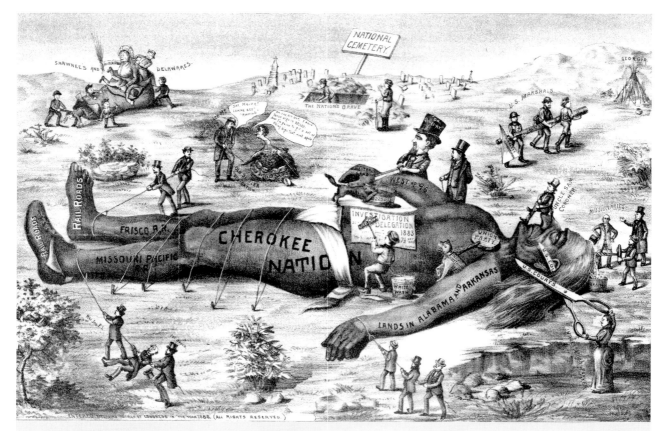

Caricature showing the despoiling of the Cherokee Nation (1886)

clear language of the 1866 treaty, the Supreme Court ruled in the *Cherokee Tobacco* case that Cherokees were required to pay taxes on all their tobacco sales.

Justice Noah Swayne held that applying the 1868 Revenue Act to the Cherokee Nation did conflict with the 1866 treaty. Nevertheless, Justice Swayne said that "an act of Congress may supersede a prior treaty." If this creates a wrong, he wrote, then "the power of redress is with Congress, not with the judiciary. . . ."

About the same time as the *Cherokee Tobacco* decision, Congress passed a law stating that Indian tribes would no longer be recognized as independent nations with which the United States could make treaties. This law, together with the *Cherokee Tobacco* decision, meant that the remaining sovereignty of all Indian nations, including that of the Cherokee Nation, was subject to the vacillations of Congress. In other words, if Congress passed a law that violated a provision of a treaty, the only recourse that an Indian tribe would have would be to ask Congress to repeal the law; they could not look to the Supreme Court for aid. Congress, of course, had little incentive to protect Indian sovereignty when it conflicted with the demands of the ever expanding white society.

In 1887, Congress passed the Dawes General Allotment Act. This act broke up most tribally owned lands by allotting 160 acres to each head of household and 40 to 80 acres to all others. The "surplus" land remaining after allotment was opened up to whites for settlement. By the time the allotment policy was ended in 1934, over two-thirds of Native American land had become the property of white settlers, corporations, or the federal government (to be used as national parks and forests).

The Dawes Act excluded the Five Civilized Tribes (Cherokee, Chickasaw, Choctaw, Seminole, and Creek) from its provisions. But the Five Tribes still weren't safe. In 1898, Congress simply terminated the legal existence of the Five Civilized Tribes by passing the Curtis Act. The United States had tried for several years to negotiate agreements with the Five Tribes to distribute their land to individual members. The tribes didn't want this. The congressional House Committee on Indian Affairs admitted that the United States had granted these tribes legal title and that the lands could not be taken away from them without their consent. Still, it justified the Curtis Act, which was vigorously opposed by these tribes, by stating:

There are about 20 million acres of land thus owned [by the Five Tribes].

It is rich in mineral deposits, and contains a large area of splendid farming and grazing land. . . . In view of the fact that it is now impossible to secure agreements with the tribes, and the fact that the title is in the tribe, [the] committee has provided for the allotment of the . . . lands of each of the nations. . . .

In 1907, the state of Oklahoma was admitted to the Union, and without their consent, the members of the Five Tribes became citizens of Oklahoma. By 1924, most Native Americans had become citizens. Often citizenship was imposed on them by the federal government against their will. Nevertheless, they were still considered wards of the United States, with diminished rights. Conflict continues to this day over Indian rights and land.

In essence, the United States stole, bought, or acquired by bribery the lands populated by many Native American nations before the arrival of whites. Hundreds of Indian tribes were decimated, and most lost their traditional means of survival. The high poverty and unemployment rates among Native Americans today are the direct result of the seizure of their lands by white society and the destruction of their way of life.

"Beings of an Inferior Order": Can African Americans Ever Be Citizens?

3

The Constitution Says . . .
"The judicial Power shall extend . . . to Controversies . . . between Citizens of different States. . . ."
—U.S. Constitution, Article III, Section 2, Clause 1

"The Citizens of each State shall be entitled to all Privileges and Immunities of Citizens in the several States."
—U.S. Constitution, Article IV, Section 2, Clause 1

"The Congress shall have Power to dispose of and make all needful Rules and Regulations respecting the Territory . . . belonging to the United States. . . ."
—U.S. Constitution, Article IV, Section 3, Clause 2

Illustration from the *American Anti-Slavery Almanac* for 1840

By the mid-nineteenth century, the United States had tripled in size and population. Through purchase, treaty, or conquest, the nation's borders now stretched from the Atlantic to the Pacific oceans. The forced removal of the Indians from the South had opened up rich agricultural land for development. Plantations in Mississippi, Alabama, and Georgia sprang up like mushrooms. In 1845, Texas became a state, and in 1848, most of what is now California,

Northern Hospitality—New-York nine months law. [The Slave steps out of the Slave State, and his chains fall. A Free State, with another chain, stands ready to re-enslave him.]

Burning of McIntosh at St. Louis, in April, 1836.

Showing how slavery improves the condition of the female sex.

The Negro Pew, or "Free" Seats for black Christians. | *Mayor of New-York refusing a Carman's license to a colored Man.*

Servility of the Northern States in arresting and returning fugitive Slaves.

Selling a Mother from her Child.

Hunting Slaves with dogs and guns. A Slave drowned by the dogs.

" Poor things, ' they can't take care of themselves.' "

Mothers with young Children at work in the field.

A Woman chained to a Girl, and a Man in irons at work in the field.

Branding Slaves.

Cutting up a Slave in Kentucky.

Paid. | *Unpaid.*

Illustrations from the *American Anti-Slavery Almanac* for 1840

19

In response to several slave uprisings and increased efforts by abolitionists to end slavery, white Southerners began in the 1830s and 1840s to push for the passage of laws, often called Black Codes, that limited the rights of free blacks and stiffened the laws governing slaves. For example, since most of the slave rebels were illiterate, Southern legislatures quickly passed laws making it illegal to teach slaves how to read and write. In a more insidious way, slaveholders also began promoting the racist ideology that Africans were inferior beings destined to be servants of the white race.

Meanwhile, as slavery became more and more entrenched in the South, the antislavery movement took hold in the North. It took on many forms—some legal and some not. The Underground Railroad was a direct response to the Fugitive Slave Clause in Article IV of the Constitution. This network was neither underground nor a railroad. Its name was a metaphor for a well-organized secret group (railroad) of people (conductors) who helped slaves escape by leading them from one safe place (station) to another. Thousands of slaves escaped to freedom via the Underground Railroad.

New Mexico, Arizona, Nevada, Utah, and Colorado was acquired by the United States from Mexico with the Treaty of Guadalupe Hidalgo, which ended the Mexican-American War. The great western lands offered seemingly unlimited opportunities and wealth to settlers, especially when gold was discovered in California in 1849.

By midcentury, the conflict over slavery was threatening to rip the nation apart. Whether a state would be admitted to the Union as slave or free became the hottest political issue of the times, and neither side was willing to compromise. It was in this climate of political and social turmoil

that the well-known *Dred Scott* case began. Even though the actual shots that began the Civil War were not fired until April 1861, some historians claim that the *Dred Scott* case was the first "battle" in the Civil War.

Attitudes about slavery had changed and intensified since the Constitution was drafted. When the nation was founded, most Southern politicians considered slavery an unfortunate evil that would eventually wither away. But the invention of the cotton gin in 1793 increased the demand for cotton and slaves. Although Congress abolished the importation of slaves from overseas in 1808, the slave trade continued nonetheless. The demand for slaves in the cotton-growing South was increasing exponentially. Plantation owners continued to import slaves illegally from Brazil and the Caribbean islands, in addition to buying slaves from other slaveholding states. Even Southerners who weren't slaveowners supported the system vigorously because they profited from it in some way. Many people who couldn't afford slaves saw no harm in others owning them.

The historic *Dred Scott* case began in Missouri, a slave state. Missouri was formed from land acquired in the Louisiana Purchase of 1803. When Missouri petitioned to join the Union in 1819, territory leaders wanted Missouri to be admitted as a slave state. This set off a vigorous debate between slavery advocates and abolitionists. Slaveholders argued that slaves were property that could be taken from place to place like farm animals or household goods. Abolitionists, on the other hand, disagreed on the grounds that human beings had a right to be free. They called for the immediate emancipation of slaves and a ban on all slavery in the western territories. Tensions between the opposing sides mounted.

Eventually, in 1820, Congress approved the Missouri Compromise. Slavery would be prohibited in the Louisiana Territory north of latitude 36° 30'—known as the Mason-Dixon Line—except for Missouri, which would be allowed to choose. The constitution of the new state of Missouri allowed slavery. Maine was accepted into the Union as a free state and Missouri was admitted as a slave state. For the time being, the Missouri Compromise calmed tempers, and both sides of the slave issue continued to be equally represented in the Senate.

Southerners hated the Missouri Compromise and argued that Congress did not have any power to regulate slavery in the territories of the Louisiana Purchase. Senator John C. Calhoun from South Carolina became the leading proponent of this position. By the 1840s, he and many other Southerners stepped up their attacks, stating that it was unconstitutional for Congress to prohibit slaveholders from emigrating into the territories with their "property" (in other words, slaves).

In 1830, Peter Blow moved to Missouri with his family and six slaves, including Dred Scott. Some time after Dred Scott moved to Missouri with the Blow family, he was sold to a physician, Dr. John Emerson. In 1833, Dr. Emerson was granted a com-

Harriet Tubman was a slave who escaped in 1849 and became a famous "conductor" on the Underground Railroad, leading more than three hundred slaves to freedom (1911).

21

mission as an assistant surgeon in the U.S. Army, and he was sent to Fort Armstrong in Rock Island, Illinois, in free territory. Although the Illinois state constitution did not allow slavery, Scott lived there as Dr. Emerson's slave.

In 1836, the Army transferred Dr. Emerson to Fort Snelling in Wisconsin Territory, which was also free, as agreed in the Missouri Compromise. Dr. Emerson took Scott with him. While there, Scott met Harriet Robinson, a slave of Major Lawrence Taliaferro, a Virginian who had brought Robinson and his other slaves to

Portrait of Dred Scott by Louis Schultze (1882)

joined them in 1842. A year later, Emerson died. Shortly thereafter, Mrs. Emerson loaned the Scotts to her brother-in-law, Captain Henry Bainbridge, who immediately hired them out to Samuel and Adeline Russell, who also lived in St. Louis. In 1846, Scott tried to buy his freedom from Mrs. Emerson, but she refused.

Were the Scotts free because they had lived in a free state? According to previous Missouri Supreme Court decisions, or precedents, the Scotts were entitled to their freedom because they had lived in free territory. But the climate had changed by the time the Scotts filed their lawsuit.

On April 6, 1846, Dred and Harriet Scott filed the first of many petitions for freedom in the Missouri Circuit Court in St. Louis. The Scotts won their suit at the trial-court level in 1850, thirty years after the Missouri Compromise.

Mrs. Emerson's attorney appealed the decision to the Missouri Supreme Court, which ruled against the Scotts. In a two-to-one decision rendered in 1851, the Missouri Supreme Court refused to follow its previous decisions. It wrote that it should not approve anything that gratified the "dark and fell spirit" that opposed slavery and "whose inevitable consequence must be the overthrow and destruction of our government."

The Missouri Supreme Court ended its decision with an incredible defense of slavery as, in fact, being good for blacks:

> As to the consequences of slavery, they are much more hurtful to the master than the slave. There is no

his Indian agency near Fort Snelling. Dred Scott and Harriet Robinson were married, and Emerson bought Harriet from Taliaferro.

Emerson was then transferred to Fort Jesup in Louisiana, a slave state, where he married Irene Sanford. Shortly after their marriage, he was transferred back to Fort Snelling, Wisconsin. Dred and Harriet Scott traveled northward with John and Irene Emerson. In 1838, while their steamboat was on the Mississippi River, north of the state of Missouri and therefore in free territory, Harriet Scott gave birth to a daughter named Eliza.

In 1840, the Scotts returned with Mrs. Emerson to St. Louis, Missouri, and Emerson

comparison between the slave in the United States and the cruel, uncivilized negro in Africa. When the condition of our slaves is contrasted with the state of their miserable race in Africa; when their civilization, intelligence and instruction in religious truths are considered, and the means now employed to restore them to the country from which they have been torn, bearing with them the blessings of civilized life, we are almost persuaded, that the introduction of slavery amongst us was, in the providence of God, who makes the evil passions of men subservient to His own glory, a means of placing that unhappy race within the pale of civilized nations.

Even though the Scotts had lost the case, the situation was not hopeless. Their lawyer decided to bring a new lawsuit against the Scotts' new owner, this time in federal court. In 1853, when the suit was filed, the Scotts had been sold by Mrs. Emerson to John Sanford, who lived in New York. Article III, Section 2, Clause 1 of the Constitution gives the federal courts the power to rule on suits between citizens of different states. The Scotts' lawyer argued that the federal courts had the power to hear the dispute because Dred Scott was a citizen of Missouri while Sanford was a citizen of New York.

The Scotts were allowed to be heard in federal court, but they lost the case. They appealed to the U.S. Supreme Court, which agreed to hear the case. Sanford's

If Dred Scott had sued for his freedom in 1833, when Dr. Emerson took him to Illinois, or in 1836, when he was taken to the Wisconsin Territory, or even in 1840, when he returned to Missouri, he and his family almost certainly would have been free within a short time. However, by the 1850s, when the Missouri Supreme Court and then the U.S. Supreme Court decided his case, Southern leaders had become far more sophisticated in their defense of slavery. Dred and Harriet Scott became caught in the crosswinds of political change.

attorney argued that blacks were not citizens and couldn't sue in federal court. He also attacked the constitutionality of the Missouri Compromise. Chief Justice Roger Taney wrote the opinion for the Court, which ruled in 1857 against the Scotts in a five-to-four decision.

Chief Justice Taney bypassed Article III, Section 2, Clause 1 in making his decision and based his opinion on Article IV, Section 2, Clause 1. It states, "The Citizens of each State shall be entitled to all Privileges and Immunities of Citizens in the several States."

Chief Justice Taney framed the issue in this way:

The question is simply this: Can a negro, whose ancestors were imported into this country and sold as slaves, become a member of the political community formed and brought into existence by the Constitution of the United States, and as such become entitled to all the rights, and privileges, and immunities, guarant[e]ed by that instrument to the

23

citizen. One of these rights is the privilege of suing in a court of the United States in the cases specified in the Constitution.

Chief Justice Taney's answer to the citizenship question was a resounding "no!" He claimed:

- Blacks were not citizens of any of the states that adopted the Constitution in 1789.

- The framers of the Constitution did not consider free blacks to be citizens under the Constitution.

- Therefore, blacks could not be considered citizens in 1857.

24 Chief Justice Taney claimed that the condition of blacks at the time of the adoption of the Constitution was the following:

[Negroes] had for more than a century before been regarded as beings of an inferior order, and altogether unfit to associate with the white race, either in social or political relations; and so far inferior, that they had no rights which the white man was bound to respect; and that the negro might justly and lawfully be reduced to slavery for his benefit. He was bought and sold, and treated as an ordinary article of merchandise and traffic, whenever a profit could be made by it. This opinion was at that time fixed and universal in the civilized portion of the white race.

Engraving of Chief Justice Roger B. Taney (circa 1850)

As Justice Benjamin Curtis pointed out in his dissent, this was a flagrant misstatement of the situation of free African Americans in the United States in 1789. Five states at that time considered free blacks to be citizens. Although few in number, they could even vote under some of the early state constitutions. They also could marry, sign contracts, buy and sell real estate, file suit in courts, and will their property. So even where they did not have the right to vote, they did have other rights "which the white man was bound to respect." In some regards, their rights in 1789 exceeded those of married white women, whom Chief Justice Taney did consider to be citizens.

Chief Justice Taney also claimed that the categories of people who could be citizens of the United States were fixed at the time of the adoption of the Constitution. He ruled that even if a state recognized free blacks as citizens, this did not make them citizens of the United States. They would have the rights provided to them under the laws and constitution of the state in which they resided but would have no rights under the federal Constitution.

Chief Justice Taney wrote that considering free blacks to be citizens of the United States:

> would give to persons of the negro race . . . the right to enter every other State whenever they pleased, singly or in companies, without pass or passport, and without obstruction, to

Woodcut depicting Nat Turner's rebellion (1831)

sojourn there as long as they pleased, to go where they pleased at every hour of the day or night without molestation, unless they committed some violation of law for which a white man would be punished; and it would give them the full liberty of speech in public and in private upon all subjects upon which its own citizens might speak; to hold public meetings upon political affairs, and to keep and carry arms wherever they went. And all of this would be done in the face of the subject race of the same color, both free and slaves, inevitably producing discontent and insubordination among them, and endangering the peace and safety of the State.

Chief Justice Taney wrote: "[A]n Act of Congress which deprives a citizen of the United States of his liberty or property, merely because he came himself or brought his property into a particular Territory of the United States . . . could hardly be dignified with the name of due process of law."

Chief Justice Taney argued that treating free blacks as citizens threatened the security of slave-holding states, as free blacks would be able to organize and by example lead enslaved blacks to demand their freedom as well. His conclusion was that blacks can "claim none of the rights and privileges which [the Constitution] provides for and secures to citizens of the United States."

This decision could have ended with his conclusion that Dred Scott was not, and never could be, a citizen. For if that were the case, Scott had no right to sue in federal court and the *Scott* case would be dismissed. But the Court voted to take on the question of the Missouri Compromise, so Chief Justice Taney plunged into that issue as well. He used the opportunity to establish broad rights for slaveholders in territories acquired by the United States.

This part of the decision required Chief Justice Taney to interpret Article IV, Section 3, Clause 2 of the Constitution: "The Congress shall have Power to dispose of and make all needful Rules and Regulations respecting the Territory or other Property belonging to the United States. . . ."

This clause seems to allow Congress to pass laws to govern U.S. territories. The very first Congress in 1789 readopted the Northwest Ordinance, passed by the Continental Congress in 1787, which established the governmental structure of the territory north of the Ohio River and which prohibited slavery in that territory. As the United States acquired other territories, Congress routinely passed laws regulating a variety of matters in these territories, including contracts, wills, marriage, gambling, dueling, crime, criminal procedures, and slavery. Chief Justice Marshall, in an 1828 case, said this clause meant that Congress could govern the territories that existed in 1788 when the Constitution was adopted, as well as territories that the United States acquired afterward. (Citizens of a territory could apply for statehood once the population reached

60,000 habitants.)

Chief Justice Taney, however, interpreted the clause to mean *only* the territory that was owned by the United States in 1789. While Chief Justice Taney acknowledged that Congress could pass some regulations concerning territories, he said Congress could not pass any laws restricting slavery, because this would amount to a deprivation of property (slaves) without due process of law, in violation of the Fifth Amendment. He therefore declared the Missouri Compromise to be unconstitutional.

Dred and Harriet Scott and their family had lost. So had every other black person in the United States, whether slave or free, for the Supreme Court had ruled that no black person could ever become a citizen of the United States.

The Scotts did obtain their freedom shortly after the decision. John Sanford, the defendant in the *Dred Scott* case, died in May 1857. Shortly thereafter, Mrs. Emerson (now Chaffee) and her husband (a Republican Congressman from Massachusetts) signed a deed transferring ownership of the Scott family to Taylor Blow (son of Dred Scott's owner in 1830), who promptly emancipated them on May 26, 1857.

Dred Scott enjoyed freedom for little more than a year. He died on September 17, 1858. Not much is known about Harriet Scott after her husband's death. One account says "she died a few years after Dred" but before Eliza, who "died in 1862 at the age of twenty-five."

The *Dred Scott* judgment, written by Chief Justice Taney in 1857

"ENFORCED SEPARATION OF THE RACES": CAN CITIZENS BE SEGREGATED BY RACE?

THE CONSTITUTION SAYS . . .

"NEITHER SLAVERY NOR INVOLUNTARY SERVITUDE, EXCEPT AS A PUNISHMENT FOR CRIME WHEREOF THE PARTY SHALL HAVE BEEN DULY CONVICTED, SHALL EXIST WITHIN THE UNITED STATES, OR ANY PLACE SUBJECT TO THEIR JURISDICTION."
—U.S. CONSTITUTION, AMENDMENT XIII, SECTION 1

"ALL PERSONS BORN OR NATURALIZED IN THE UNITED STATES, AND SUBJECT TO THE JURISDICTION THEREOF, ARE CITIZENS OF THE UNITED STATES AND OF THE STATE WHEREIN THEY RESIDE. NO STATE SHALL MAKE OR ENFORCE ANY LAW WHICH SHALL ABRIDGE THE PRIVILEGES OR IMMUNITIES OF CITIZENS OF THE UNITED STATES; NOR SHALL ANY STATE DEPRIVE ANY PERSON OF LIFE, LIBERTY, OR PROPERTY, WITHOUT DUE PROCESS OF LAW; NOR DENY TO ANY PERSON WITHIN ITS JURISDICTION THE EQUAL PROTECTION OF THE LAWS."
—U.S. CONSTITUTION, AMENDMENT XIV, SECTION 1

"THE RIGHT OF CITIZENS OF THE UNITED STATES TO VOTE SHALL NOT BE DENIED OR ABRIDGED BY THE UNITED STATES OR BY ANY STATE ON ACCOUNT OF RACE, COLOR, OR PREVIOUS CONDITION OF SERVITUDE."
—U.S. CONSTITUTION, AMENDMENT XV, SECTION 1

4

Abraham Lincoln (1863)

Charleston, South Carolina, bay.

When the war began, Lincoln's primary goal was to preserve the Union. Since there were four slaveholding states among the twenty-three states (out of a total of thirty-four) that remained in the Union—Maryland, Missouri, Kentucky, and Delaware—Lincoln didn't want to risk driving them to secession by attacking slavery.

Abolitionists and Republican congressional leaders pressed for the immediate emancipation of the slaves. But it wasn't until Lincoln was convinced that emancipation would strengthen and preserve the Union that he issued an executive order, effective January 1, 1863, freeing slaves in the rebel states. Slaves living in the border states of Maryland, Missouri, Kentucky, and Delaware remained enslaved until passage of the Thirteenth Amendment two years later.

Lincoln's Emancipation Proclamation was harshly criticized by abolitionists as a halfhearted gesture that fell far short of total freedom. In part, the criticism of the Emancipation Proclamation was justified, because Lincoln's authority was not recognized in the rebel states and no slaveholder felt bound to honor the "enemy's" order. Because of the wording in the Constitution, the only way to end slavery officially was by an amendment. President Lincoln issued the proclamation as commander in chief of the Union Army; freeing the slaves was a military strategy intended to deny the South one of its largest resources—forced free labor. But the freeing of the slaves was not a totally meaningless endeavor. According to historian

The *Dred Scott* decision stopped Congress from outlawing slavery in the new western territories. It also meant that blacks—free or slave—could not vote or enjoy any rights of citizenship in the United States. Only another Supreme Court decision or an amendment to the Constitution could change the *Dred Scott* decision. Unfortunately, it would take a civil war to bring about those changes.

In November 1860, Abraham Lincoln of the radical Republican Party was elected president. By Christmas of that year, South Carolina seceded from the Union, as it had threatened to do if Lincoln was elected. Other Southern states followed, and in April 1861, the first shots of the Civil War were fired at Fort Sumter in the

John Hope Franklin, the Emancipation Proclamation gave new significance and direction to the war. It also paved the way for the Thirteenth Amendment.

In January 1865, when the Civil War was almost over, Representative Thaddeus Stevens and Senator Charles Sumner led the efforts in Congress to pass the Thirteenth Amendment to end slavery throughout the United States.

In December of the same year, the Thirteenth Amendment was ratified. Rebel states were readmitted to the Union under the condition that they ratify the amendment. Ratification of the Thirteenth Amendment meant the proslavery part of the *Dred Scott* decision was overturned.

Complete freedom at last! It was a time of great celebration. After many years of struggle, conflict, and war, the issue of slavery seemed to be resolved. Or was it?

The euphoria of being free soon wore off when the newly freed slaves realized that they had no money, no education, no jobs, and nowhere to go. In March 1865, before ratification of the Thirteenth Amendment was complete, Congress created the Freedmen's Bureau to protect the rights of former slaves and to make the transition to freedom as smooth as possible.

Meanwhile, Southern legislatures began adopting new laws called Black Codes, which were designed to find legal means to get around the Thirteenth Amendment and to keep blacks enslaved. The codes prohibited free African Americans from testifying against whites in court, serving on juries, and taking jobs that white men wanted, even if the black man was more qualified.

One of the Black Codes allowed unemployed blacks to be arrested as vagrants and given unusually long jail sentences. Then they were forced to work for landowners (many of whom were former slaveowners) or to work on public works projects for free. In some states, newly freed slaves who failed to do what their employers

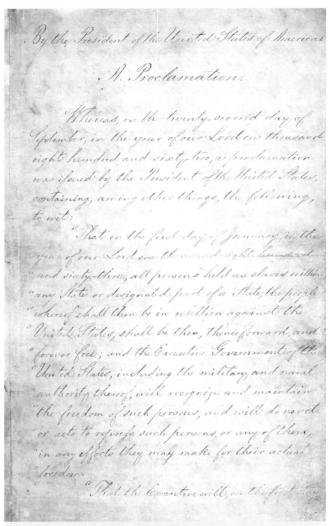

The Emancipation Proclamation (1863)

Gathering of the Freedmen's Bureau, Beaufort, South Carolina (1870s)

demanded, or who simply missed work, could be arrested, fined, and ordered back to work by a judge.

In response to the Black Codes, Congress proposed the Fourteenth Amendment in 1866. It overturned the *Dred Scott* decision, making all blacks and others born in the country citizens. It also prohibited states from denying their citizens equal protection under the law. By July 1868, twenty-eight out of thirty-seven states, including four Southern states, had ratified the Fourteenth Amendment, and it became part of the Constitution. There remained, however, the question of voting rights. By 1868, only eight states allowed African American men to vote.

In February 1869, Congress sent the Fifteenth Amendment, which guaranteed African American *men* the right to vote, to the states for ratification. The states barely ratified the amendment in early 1870, and only because Congress required Southern states that had not yet been readmitted

to the Union to ratify the Fifteenth
Amendment, as well as the Fourteenth
Amendment, as a condition of readmis-
sion.

With these three new amendments,
legal equality for African Americans—at
least African American men—seemed to be
firmly in place as a constitutional matter.

The mood of the country had shifted by
the 1876 presidential election. With strong
legislation in place, many whites felt there
was no more need to give former slaves
special attention. Blacks were expected—
and they were willing—to take their places
alongside their fellow American citizens.
The country turned toward the southwest,
where it was poised once again to fight the
Indians for control of land.

As he had promised during a post-
election electoral dispute, President
Rutherford B. Hayes pulled the last federal
troops out of the South in 1877. Now the
South was free to pursue its own policies
with regard to race. Without military protection, blacks lost most of the rights they
had been granted by the constitutional
amendments.

Just as important, the Supreme Court
itself, through its interpretations of
post–Civil War amendments, played a key
role in allowing racial apartheid to be firmly
in place by the turn of the century.

In 1873, the Supreme Court gave a narrow interpretation to the Fourteenth Amendment. The Court ruled that it was up to the
states, not the federal government, to protect most of the privileges and immunities
of citizenship.

In 1877, in a shocking decision, the
High Court overturned an 1869 Louisiana
state law that prohibited segregation in
public transportation. The majority of the
justices ruled that Louisiana's law violated
the Constitution by interfering with inter-

state commerce. They said that under the Commerce Clause of the Constitution, only Congress could regulate interstate commerce. Although Congress had just prohibited discrimination in public accommodations and transportation, the Supreme Court ruled that companies were free to adopt any "reasonable rules" pertaining to passengers that they felt to be in the best interest of all concerned.

The 1877 decision gave a green light to apartheid. All over the country, states passed laws segregating blacks and whites.

The laws forbade interracial marriages. They established separate schools, hospitals, even cemeteries.

The Supreme Court further restricted blacks' rights in two 1883 rulings. First, the Court unanimously upheld Alabama's law forbidding interracial marriages, ruling that it did not violate the Fourteenth Amendment's Equal Protection Clause.

Then the Court ruled that the Fourteenth Amendment didn't authorize Congress to pass the 1875 Civil Rights Act, which guaranteed equal rights in public

"Visit of the Ku-Klux" drawing by Frank Bellew (1872)

accommodations. It held that the Fourteenth Amendment only prohibited *states*, not *individuals*, from denying citizens equal protection of the law.

In 1890, the Supreme Court upheld a state law in Mississippi that required segregation on all trains operating within Mississippi. It ruled that Mississippi's law did not violate the Commerce Clause.

Within a few months of the Mississippi segregation decision, Louisiana passed its own railroad-segregation law, the Separate Car Act. The law required "equal, but separate" accommodations in Louisiana for whites and blacks on railroads (but not on streetcars). When a special car was not provided, blacks sat in the back while whites rode in the front. The only exception was made for black "nurses attending children of the other race."

As soon as the law passed, a group of black professionals in New Orleans formed the Citizens' Committee to Test the Constitutionality of the Separate Car Law.

They developed a plan to file a test case challenging the new law. They looked for a willing plaintiff, as well as a railroad that would cooperate with them in setting up an arrest of the plaintiff.

The committee found its best test plaintiff in Homer Plessy. His maternal great-grandmother was black; therefore, he was only one-eighth "black" and seven-eighths "white." For all practical purposes, he looked white. According to the Black Codes, any person who had any "black blood" was considered black.

In June 1892, Plessy took a seat in a Louisiana railroad car designated for whites only. The conductor could not tell whether Plessy was white or not, so Plessy told him he was black. When Plessy refused to move from the white car, he was arrested and charged with violating the Separate Car Act. The attorneys for the Citizens' Committee filed motions to have Plessy's charges dismissed.

Both the trial judge and the Louisiana Supreme Court upheld the law. The attorneys appealed the case to the U.S. Supreme Court. The heart of their argument was that it was unconstitutional for the state to label and divide citizens by color. They pointed out that the goal of the law was "to separate the Negroes from the whites in public conveyances for the gratification and recognition of the sentiment of white superiority and white supremacy of right and power." The law therefore infringed upon the equal rights guaranteed by the Fourteenth Amendment.

Plessy's attorneys also argued that allowing train conductors to decide the

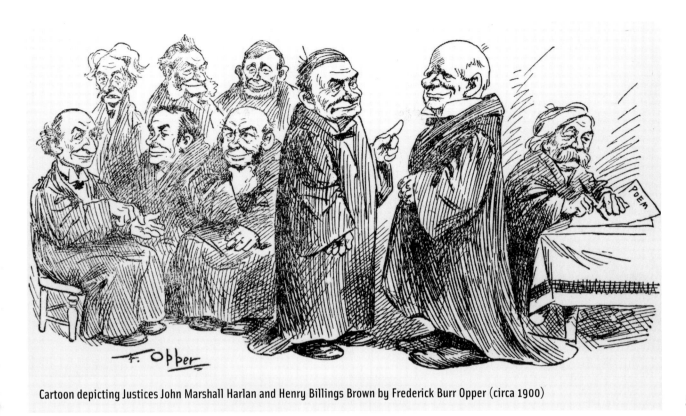

Cartoon depicting Justices John Marshall Harlan and Henry Billings Brown by Frederick Burr Opper (circa 1900)

race of passengers violated the Fourteenth Amendment, depriving passengers of due process of law. They argued that reputation was a form of property. If a person was assigned to the "colored" car, he would "inevitably be regarded as a colored man or at least suspected of being one." This would further deprive a man, such as Plessy, of his reputation of being a white man. This argument was laced with the racist notion that being white is better than being black:

> How much would it be worth to a young man entering upon the practice of law, to be regarded as a *white* man rather than a colored one? Six-sevenths of the population are white. Nineteen-twentieths of the property of the country is owned by white people. Ninety-nine hundredths of the business opportunities are in the control of white people. These propositions are rendered even more startling by the intensity of feeling which excludes the colored man from the friendship and companionship of the white man. . . . Under these conditions, is it possible to conclude that the *reputation of being white* is not property? Indeed, is it not the most valuable sort of property, being the master-key that unlocks the golden door of opportunity?

Finally, Plessy's attorneys argued that the Separate Car Act violated the Thirteenth Amendment by promoting white supremacy over blacks. Mandating such submissiveness and inferior status was "the result and essential concomitant of slavery."

The Supreme Court upheld Louisiana's law by a vote of seven to one (one justice did not participate in the case). Justice Henry Billings Brown, from Massachusetts, wrote the Court's opinion. Ruling that the Constitution allowed distinctions based on color, he wrote:

> A statute which implies merely a legal distinction between the white and colored races—a distinction which is founded in the color of the two races, and which must always exist so long as white men are distinguished from the other race by color—has no tendency to destroy the legal equality of the two races, or re-establish a state of involuntary servitude.

The Court assumed in its decision that it was clear who was "white" and who was "colored," as if race had a scientific or legal meaning. Yet the Louisiana Separate Car Act did not define race, and the concept of race is a matter of social, rather than scientific, definition.

As Plessy's attorneys had pointed out in their brief:

> The crime, then, for which he became liable for imprisonment . . . was that a person of seven-eighths Caucasian blood insisted on sitting peacefully and quietly in a car the state of Louisiana had commanded the company to set

aside exclusively for the white race. Where on earth should he have gone? Will the court hold that a single drop of African blood is sufficient to color a whole ocean of Caucasian whiteness?

Justice Brown concluded:

> The enforced separation of the races . . . neither abridges the privileges or immunities of the colored man, deprives him of his property without due process of laws, nor denies him the equal protection of the laws within the meaning of the Fourteenth Amendment.

In response to the argument that the Separate Car Act allowed deprivation of property—the reputation of being white—without due process, Justice Brown wrote:

> The recently completed Human Genome Sequencing Project has shown that there is no biological basis for dividing human beings into races. "The amount of divergence (differences) between humans is essentially zero," stated Joseph L. Graves Jr., an evolutionary biologist and author, in a 2002 interview with a *St. Louis Post-Dispatch* reporter. According to Graves, there is overwhelming scientific evidence to support the "nonexistence of subdivisions [races] in humans." Alan R. Templeton, a population biologist at Washington University in St. Louis, agrees: "Race is real in a political, social sense, but it's not biological." Although there is no biological basis for race, race will probably remain a way in which people are categorized, says Sheilah Clarke-Ekong, a cultural anthropologist at the University of Missouri at St. Louis. "Race is about what we look like. Race is about how the tone of our voice settles on the ear. Race is how we understand the world, which is representative of culture, among other things."

If he be a white man and assigned to a colored coach, he may have his action for damages against the company for being deprived of his so-called property. Upon the other hand, if he be a colored man and be so assigned, he has been deprived of no property, since he is not lawfully entitled to the reputation of being a white man.

Again the lone dissenter, Justice Harlan wrote:

Everyone knows that the statute in question had its origin in the purpose, not so much to exclude white persons from railroad cars occupied by blacks, as to exclude colored people from coaches occupied by or assigned to whites.

In response to the argument that segregation stamped African Americans with a "badge of inferiority," Justice Brown wrote,

"If this be so, it is not by reason of anything found in the act, but solely because the colored race chooses to put that construction upon it."

Justice Harlan responded that the *Plessy v. Ferguson* decision would:

prove to be quite as pernicious as the decision made by this tribunal in the *Dred Scott Case*. . . . What can more certainly arouse race hate, what more certainly create and perpetuate a feeling of distrust between these races [white and black], than state enactments which in fact proceed on the ground that colored citizens are so inferior and degraded that they cannot be allowed to sit in public coaches occupied by white citizens? That, as all will admit, is the real meaning of such legislation as was enacted in Louisiana. . . . The thin disguise of "equal" accommodations for passengers in railroad coaches

Although Justice Harlan had a keen understanding of racism when it involved blacks, he appeared to lack such insight when it involved Native Americans. In 1890, he ruled in *Cherokee Nation v. Kansas Railway Co.* that the United States government could grant a railroad company the right to build a railway through lands owned by the Cherokee Nation. Justice Harlan stated: "The fact that the Cherokee Nation [owns their lands] is of no consequence. . . . The lands in the Cherokee territory . . . are held subject to the authority of the general government to take them for such objects as are germane to the execution of the powers granted to it; provided only, that they are not taken without just compensation being made to the owner."

Moreover, only one week after his eloquent dissent in the *Plessy* case, Justice Harlan joined with the majority of the Supreme Court in a decision that further undermined Indian treaty rights. In *Ward v. Race Horse,* the Court upheld the right of the state of Wyoming to prosecute a Bannock Indian for exercising hunting rights that the Bannocks had been guaranteed in an 1868 treaty with the United States. The Court ruled that the hunting rights ended when Wyoming became a state, even though the treaty made no reference to statehood as a justification for terminating these treaty rights. Ironically, Justice Brown, who had written the *Plessy* decision that ushered in sixty years of legal segregation, dissented in the *Ward* case. He argued that Congress should not be able to repudiate the Bannock treaty, and that hunting was not merely a sport for the Bannocks but essential to their survival.

"Colored only" drinking fountain on county courthouse lawn, Halifax, North Carolina (1938)

will not mislead anyone, or atone for the wrong this day done.

After the *Plessy* decision, segregation laws proliferated, and "separate but equal" became a synonym for apartheid. By the turn of the century, apartheid was a way of life in America.

Within three years of the *Plessy* decision, the Supreme Court effectively eliminated even the requirement of "equal" by ruling that the Equal Protection Clause of the Fourteenth Amendment was not violated by a Georgia school district that closed its only high school for African Americans while providing a high school for whites.

As Justice Harlan noted in his dissent, the *Plessy* decision returned black citizens to one rung above slavery. It seemed to be more in accordance with the *Dred Scott* decision, which stated that blacks were not citizens and therefore "had no rights which the white man was bound to respect," than with the Thirteenth, Fourteenth, and

Fifteenth Amendments to the Constitution, which were intended to overturn *Dred Scott.*

The *Plessy* decision had a wide-sweeping effect on the American system of justice for over a half century. The High Court continued to permit segregation until 1954, almost sixty years after *Plessy.* It finally overturned the decision in 1956.

39

"The Respective Spheres and Destinies of Man and Woman": Should Women Have the Same Rights as Men?

The Constitution Says . . .

"The Citizens of each State shall be entitled to all Privileges and Immunities of Citizens in the several States."

—U.S. Constitution, Article IV, Section 2, Clause 1

"No State shall make or enforce any law which shall abridge the privileges or immunities of citizens of the United States; nor shall any State deprive any person of life, liberty, or property, without due process of law; nor deny to any person within its jurisdiction the equal protection of the laws."

—U.S. Constitution, Amendment XIV, Section 1

"The right of citizens of the United States to vote shall not be denied or abridged by the United States or by any State on account of sex."

—U.S. Constitution, Amendment XIX

5

Julia Ward Howe (1908)

Susan B. Anthony (1871)

The early feminists, such as Julia Ward Howe, Susan B. Anthony, and Sojourner Truth, were among the strongest supporters of the abolitionist movement. After slavery was abolished, women championed the passage of the Thirteenth and Fourteenth Amendments. But women were stunned and outraged when they were not also granted the right to vote.

In response, Susan B. Anthony, the president of the American Equal Rights Association, registered and voted in the 1872 presidential election in Rochester, New York. At that time, it was a federal crime to vote knowing that it was illegal. Anthony was arrested and vigorously prosecuted for voting. But she argued that one of the privi-

leges of citizenship was the right to vote, and that the Fourteenth Amendment prohibited abridging the privileges of citizens; therefore, she didn't break the law. The judge refused to allow Anthony to testify, saying she was "incompetent" to do so because she was a woman. He ordered the jury to find her guilty. He imposed a $100 fine and court costs. She refused to pay. Following her arrest, Anthony gave a speech in which she asked, "Is it a crime for a citizen to vote?" That became the cornerstone of the women's suffrage argument.

In 1872, Virginia Minor, president of the Missouri Woman Suffrage Association, tried to register to vote in St. Louis County, Missouri, but was turned down. The

Sojourner Truth (1864)

women) provided for in the original Constitution (Article IV, Section 2). The Court said states had the right to set voting regulations. It concluded that "the Constitution of the United States does not confer the right of suffrage upon anyone, and that the constitutions and laws of the several States which commit that important trust to men alone are not necessarily void." Although it was not the intent at the time, this decision was used later to support the literacy tests and grandfather clauses that restricted blacks' right to vote.

Blocked by the Court's decision, women could obtain the right to vote only by constitutional amendment, a long and exhausting effort that was not successful until 1920.

Meanwhile, women pressed for equal rights on other fronts. Thirty-eight-year-old Myra Bradwell had been assisting her husband, James Bradwell, in his law firm since the 1850s. Her work had sparked her interest in becoming a licensed lawyer. In 1868, she started the *Chicago Legal News,* which became a well-respected legal journal. The following year, she passed the Illinois bar examination with honors and sought a license to practice law from the Illinois Supreme Court.

Despite these impressive credentials, the Illinois Supreme Court refused to admit her. The justices used a legal concept called "coverture" that says married women have no legal existence. They said that because of "the disability imposed by [her] married condition," she wouldn't be bound by any contracts she made, including contracts made as a lawyer.

Bradwell submitted a supplemental

Missouri constitution said that only men could vote. Minor, together with her husband, then brought suit challenging the law. They argued that the law breached her privileges and immunities as a citizen, in violation of the Fourteenth Amendment.

In 1875, the Supreme Court ruled unanimously against Minor in *Minor v. Happersett.* Chief Justice Morrison R. Waite wrote that the Fourteenth Amendment "did not add to the privileges and immunities" of citizens (including

> Coverture, developed by English courts of common law during the Middle Ages, was a legal principle that a husband and wife were considered one person. William Blackstone, a famous commentator on the laws of England, wrote in the eighteenth century: "[T]he very being or legal existence of the woman is suspended during the marriage, or at least is incorporated and consolidated into that of the husband: under whose wing, protection and *cover,* she performs every thing . . . and her condition during her marriage is called her *coverture.* . . . And, therefore, all deeds executed, and acts done, by her, during her coverture, are void, or at least voidable. . . ."

brief to the court, showing that coverture no longer applied in Illinois. She argued that it was "neither a crime nor a disqualification to be a married woman."

The Illinois Supreme Court reconsidered its decision. Although it acknowledged that Bradwell's brief was well written and her qualifications impeccable, it still refused to grant her a license. This time, the court used simply the fact that she was a woman. Whether she was married or single didn't matter. Although Illinois law stated that any qualified adult could be admitted to practice law, the court concluded that because the Illinois statute did not explicitly state that women could be lawyers, this meant that women should not be allowed to practice law. The court was concerned that the intensity and conflict involved in a law practice would "tend to destroy the deference and delicacy with which it is a matter of pride of our ruder sex to treat [women]," and worried about the effect of women lawyers on the "administration of justice." It noted that if women

could practice law, then they might also become governors and sheriffs.

Denouncing the Illinois Supreme Court's decision as "annihilating the political rights of women in the same manner that the *Dred Scott* decision had annihilated the citizenship rights of blacks," Bradwell asked the U.S. Supreme Court to hear the case. She hired Matthew H. Carpenter, a senator from Wisconsin, who was known for being a constitutional-law scholar and an advocate of women's equality, to represent her. Carpenter was representing the state of Louisiana in another suit called the *Slaughterhouse Cases.* The two cases were argued to the justices within a few weeks of each other in 1873. The High Court ruled against Myra Bradwell, in an eight-to-one judgment. Only Chief Justice Salmon P. Chase, a distant cousin of Bradwell's, dissented, without writing an opinion.

43

> The *Slaughterhouse Cases* involved a challenge to a New Orleans law that closed all slaughterhouses except for one. Butchers filed suit, saying that setting up a slaughterhouse monopoly violated their rights as citizens to work as butchers. Senator Carpenter argued on behalf of Louisiana against the butchers. He argued that the Fourteenth Amendment didn't expand the privileges and immunities of citizens originally granted by the Constitution under Article IV, Section 2.
>
> However, in the *Bradwell* case, Senator Carpenter argued that the Fourteenth Amendment citizenship provisions meant that every profession is open to every citizen of the United States, "male or female, black or white, married or single," and that "intelligence, integrity, and honor" are the only qualifications that can be required for employment.

The Supreme Court of the United States, posed left to right: Justice Bradley, Justice Blatchford, Justice Miller, Justice Matthews, Chief Justice Waite, Justice Gray, Justice Field, Justice Lamar, Justice Harlan (1888)

Relying on common nineteenth-century stereotypes about women and men, Justice Bradley wrote an infamous concurring opinion in *Bradwell*. Here is a portion:

[T]he civil law, as well as nature herself, has always recognized a wide difference in the respective spheres and destinies of man and woman. Man is, or should be, woman's protector and defender. The natural and proper timidity and delicacy which belongs to the female sex evidently unfits it for many of the occupations of civil life. The constitution of the family organization, which is founded in the divine ordinance, as well as in the nature of things, indicates the domestic sphere as that which properly belongs to the domain and functions of womanhood. The harmony, not to say identity, of interests and views which belong or should belong to the family institution, is repugnant to the idea of a woman adopting a distinct and independent career from that of her husband. . . . [A] married woman is incapable, without her husband's consent, of making contracts which shall be binding on her or him. . . . The paramount destiny and mission of woman are to fulfill the noble and benign offices of wife and mother. This is the law of the Creator. And the rules of civil society must be adapted to the general constitution of things, and cannot be based upon exceptional cases.

Justice Samuel Miller wrote the majority opinion in the *Slaughterhouse Cases* and *Bradwell*. Both times he concluded that the Fourteenth Amendment did not grant a citizen any protection against the courts or laws of his or her own state. He also ruled in *Bradwell* that the privileges and immunities that belong to citizens of the United States do not include "the right to admission to practice [law] in the courts of a State."

Justices Joseph Bradley, Stephen Field, and Noah Swayne had dissented in the *Slaughterhouse Cases*, arguing that the right to pursue lawful employment was one of the privileges and immunities protected by the Fourteenth Amendment. Still, they voted against Bradwell in her case, saying that the privileges and immunities of *women* did not include the right to engage in every profession.

While Bradwell's case was winding its way through the courts, Alta Hulett, an eighteen-year-old woman who had studied law with a practicing attorney, applied for admission to the Illinois bar. She was, predictably, rejected by the Illinois Supreme Court in 1871. She proceeded to draft a bill

The first Native American woman attorney was Lyda Burton Conley, a descendant of the Wyandotte Indians. In 1904, she learned that Congress planned to raze an Indian burial ground, where her parents and a sister were buried, in order to make way for a commercial development project. An 1855 treaty had guaranteed that the cemetery would be preserved permanently as a Wyandotte burial ground. Lyda Conley and another sister, Helena Conley, put up barriers around the cemetery, posted a sign saying TRESPASSERS, BEWARE!, and sat with loaded guns in a six-by-eight-foot hut that they built in the cemetery. While fending off the building contractors, Lyda Conley studied law. Before she finished law school, she filed suit against the federal government, seeking a court injunction to stop the removal of the bodies from the cemetery. She eventually argued her case before the Supreme Court.

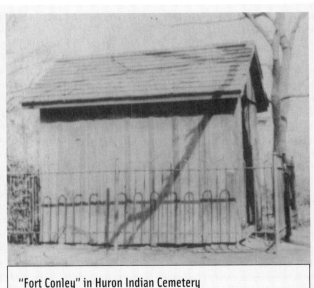

"Fort Conley" in Huron Indian Cemetery

The Supreme Court ruled unanimously against her in 1910, concluding that the United States government was bound "only by honor, not by law" to maintain the cemetery and that the Wyandotte Nation had to rely on the "good faith of the United States" to fulfill the treaty provision. In 1903, the Supreme Court had held unanimously in *Lone Wolf v. Hitchcock* that Congress had unlimited and unreviewable authority over Indian tribes, Indian treaties, and Indian property. Congress could nullify an Indian treaty whenever it chose to do so. Senator Matthew Quay, a Republican from Pennsylvania, described the 1903 decision "as the *Dred Scott* decision No. 2, except in this case the victim is red instead of black. It practically inculcates [instills] the doctrine that the red man has no rights which the white man is bound to respect, and that no treaty or contract made with him is binding." Although Conley lost the cemetery suit, Congress eventually passed a law prohibiting destruction of the cemetery.

The first black woman lawyer was Charlotte E. Ray, who graduated from Howard University Law School and was admitted to the District of Columbia bar in 1872. Unfortunately, she eventually left the practice of law due to difficulty in obtaining clients, because of both her race and sex. Another black woman, Mary Ann Shadd (later Mary Ann Cary), pictured above, had better success in her law practice. After graduating from Howard University Law School in 1883, when she was sixty years old, she went on to practice her profession until she died ten years later.

The Supreme Court did allow a woman, Belva Lockwood, to practice before the Court only six years after the *Bradwell* decision. But the Court did not change its position that *states* could deny women the right to practice law, which thirty states continued to do.

In 1874, after Lockwood was admitted to the bar in the District of Columbia, she asked the U.S. Court of Claims in Washington, D.C., to admit her to practice before that court. The Court of Claims refused, on the grounds that she was a woman. Lockwood then petitioned Congress to pass a law requiring the federal courts to allow any qualified woman, whether married or not, to practice before the courts. After rejecting the proposed bill four years in a row, Congress passed it in 1879, and President Rutherford B. Hayes signed it into law. A month later, Lockwood was admitted to practice as a lawyer before both the Court of Claims and the Supreme Court.

Meanwhile, the struggle to obtain the right to vote for women continued across the country. Wyoming Territory was the first place after the Civil War to grant women the right to vote, in 1870, followed by Utah Territory. Between 1870 and 1909, there were almost five hundred campaigns in over thirty states to get suffrage on the ballot—for male voters to decide if women should be allowed to vote. (Women, of course, could not vote in elections about matters that concerned their rights.) Only seventeen statewide votes on suffrage occurred, and only two were successful, in Colorado (in 1893) and Idaho (in 1896).

A federal constitutional amendment to

for the Illinois legislature providing that no one could be barred from any occupation, profession, or employment, except the military, on account of the person's sex. After an intensive lobbying effort by Hulett, Bradwell, and others, the Illinois legislature passed the bill. Hulett was admitted to the Illinois bar in 1872 and had a thriving law practice until her early death in 1877. Bradwell was admitted to the Illinois bar in 1890.

Members of the Woman's Christian Temperance Union (1922)

guarantee women the right to vote was first introduced in 1868, and revised in 1878. It was reintroduced almost every year until 1896, when the federal effort was dropped due to congressional opposition to women's suffrage.

The suffrage movement suddenly regained momentum in 1910, when the state of Washington approved suffrage by a two-to-one margin in a statewide vote. California followed suit the next year. Some state legislatures then began allowing women to vote in presidential elections, relying on Article II, Section 1, Clause 2

of the Constitution to argue that the states could set qualifications for voting for president.

Yet despite some success, the majority of statewide women's suffrage votes continued to be defeated. Among the biggest opponents of suffrage were the liquor interests because many women supported temperance—abstinence from alcohol.

The suffrage movement turned its energies, once again, to achieving a federal constitutional amendment. The Congressional Union (later the National Women's Party) held the Democratic Party responsible for the failure of the federal suffrage amendment. It therefore adopted the tactic of organizing to defeat Democrats in states where women could vote. In 1915, it expanded its organizing to all forty-eight states.

After Woodrow Wilson was reelected president in 1916, the National American

Suffragists marching, New York City (circa 1913)

Woman Suffrage Association, headed by Carrie Chapman Catt, focused on winning President Wilson's support for a federal constitutional amendment. President Wilson stood behind their cause by 1918. The association also developed vigorous suffrage campaigns in the thirty-six states needed to win passage of a federal constitutional

amendment (three-fourths of the states). Meanwhile, the National Women's Party adopted a militant strategy of picketing the White House.

By 1918, congressional support for suffrage had increased substantially. The amendment squeaked through the House of Representatives by a vote of 274 to 136 (274 votes was the minimum number necessary to pass the amendment in the House). Fifty-six men had changed their no vote in 1915 to yes in 1918. But the vote for suffrage in the Senate—62 to 34—was two votes short of sending the amendment to the states for ratification.

The National American Woman Suffrage Asso-

Sixty-sixth Congress of the United States of America;

At the First Session,

Begun and held at the City of Washington on Monday, the nineteenth day of May, one thousand nine hundred and nineteen.

JOINT RESOLUTION

Proposing an amendment to the Constitution extending the right of suffrage to women.

Resolved by the Senate and House of Representatives of the United States of America in Congress assembled (two-thirds of each House concurring therein), That the following article is proposed as an amendment to the Constitution, which shall be valid to all intents and purposes as part of the Constitution when ratified by the legislatures of three-fourths of the several States.

"ARTICLE ——.

"The right of citizens of the United States to vote shall not be denied or abridged by the United States or by any State on account of sex.

"Congress shall have power to enforce this article by appropriate legislation."

F. H. Gillett,
Speaker of the House of Representatives.

Thos. R. Marshall,
Vice President of the United States and
President of the Senate.

The Nineteenth Amendment to the U.S. Constitution (1920)

ciation then targeted four senators from eastern states who were up for reelection in 1918 and who had voted against suffrage. They succeeded in defeating two of them. One of the other senators barely won reelection, and the fourth won by a far lower percentage than he had in previous elections.

These efforts paid off. With 117 new members, the House repassed the amendment in May 1919—this time with a vote of 304 to 89. The Senate passed it with 66 yes votes in June 1919, two votes more than needed. Ratification of the amendment by the states took until August 18, 1920.

"THE UGLY ABYSS OF RACISM": WHAT RIGHTS DO IMMIGRANTS AND THEIR CHILDREN HAVE?

THE CONSTITUTION SAYS . . .
"NO PERSON SHALL . . . BE DEPRIVED OF LIFE, LIBERTY, OR PROPERTY, WITHOUT DUE PROCESS OF LAW. . . ."
—U.S. CONSTITUTION, AMENDMENT V

"ALL PERSONS BORN OR NATURALIZED IN THE UNITED STATES . . . ARE CITIZENS OF THE UNITED STATES AND OF THE STATE WHEREIN THEY RESIDE."
—U.S. CONSTITUTION, AMENDMENT XIV, SECTION 1

6

Immigrants at Ellis Island, New York City (1904)

Seven miners, including three white miners standing to left and four Chinese miners standing to right (1852)

The virus of racism that developed with regard to Native Americans and African Americans had, by the latter part of the nineteenth century, also infected American policies toward Asian immigrants. Some scientists developed and popularized the idea that intelligence and character were hereditary, rather than affected by educational opportunities and social and economic conditions. Behind this faulty premise was the notion that Northern and Western Europeans were inherently superior to people of color, as well as to Eastern and Southern European whites. This led to the adoption of restrictive immigration policies toward people other than Northern and Western Europeans. Decisions about who could come to America became more and more decided by race.

It was this kind of thinking that was partly responsible for the incarceration of all people of Japanese background—both immigrants and natural-born citizens—who lived on the West Coast during World War II.

Historically, racism against Asians goes back to the first naturalization law, passed by Congress in 1790. That law allowed only "free white persons" to become citizens of the United States. The 1849 California gold rush brought the first immigrants from China. The Chinese population in the United States quickly grew to 25,000, triggering white hostility toward Chinese immigrants. In 1879, California amended its constitution to deny the vote to those born in China, and to deny Chinese aliens the right to own property, testify against whites, bear arms, engage in mercantile businesses, and work in California's public works.

In 1882, Congress excluded all new Chinese immigrants for ten years and forbade any court from granting citizenship to a Chinese person; Congress renewed this exclusion in 1892 and again in 1902. These laws became known as the Chinese Exclusion Acts.

The hostility toward the Chinese was matched by that toward the Japanese. In the early 1900s, the California legislature labeled Japanese people as totally undesirable due to their character and "race habits" and called on Congress to stop Japanese immigration.

In 1917 and 1924, Congress passed two anti-Asian immigration laws. Together they barred all Asians from immigrating to the United States.

According to two decisions of the Supreme Court in the 1920s, Congress could exclude Asian immigrants already in the United States from becoming citizens. But the Fourteenth Amendment guaranteed that those *born* in the United States were automatically citizens. Thus, while Asian immigrants themselves could never have citizenship, they could be secure in the knowledge that their American-born children would.

With citizenship came certain constitutional protections, or so it would seem. But hysteria erupted after Japan bombed Pearl Harbor on December 7, 1941, and the United States entered World War II. Many were frightened and suspicious of those who looked like the enemy. People of German, Italian, and Japanese origin all suffered discrimination, but Japanese

> Despite their small population in California, Japanese Americans controlled almost half the commercial truck crops in 1941 due to their intensive methods of agricultural cultivation. As a result, they gained the hostility of white growers who resented the competition. A campaign for expulsion of Japanese Americans began picking up steam in early 1942. The Grower-Shipper Vegetable Association, a powerful force in the district of Representative Jack Anderson, had told a journalist that it wanted "to get rid of the [Japanese] for selfish reasons"—it was a matter of "whether the white man lives on the Pacific Coast or the brown man."

Americans suffered the most. Of those living in the United States in 1941, the vast majority were in California, and most of the rest in Oregon and Washington. About two-thirds of Japanese Americans had been born in the United States and therefore were citizens. The rest, born in Japan, could never become citizens and were considered aliens. Once war broke out with Japan, they were considered "enemy aliens," even if they'd lived in the United States for most of their lives. Hostility against those of Japanese descent extended to citizens as well as noncitizens.

In early 1942, the entire West Coast congressional delegation called for the expulsion of Japanese Americans—both citizens and noncitizens—from the coast, as did California attorney general Earl Warren, who later became chief justice of the Supreme Court. By early February, the demand for expulsion became an irresistible force. The government then moved with lightning speed to carry out the plans.

On February 19, 1942, President Roosevelt signed Executive Order No. 9066. It

Americans of Japanese ancestry awaiting the bus to a War Relocation Authority center (1942)

of the West Coast as military areas.

On March 18, 1942, President Roosevelt established the War Relocation Authority, whose task was to develop the program for removal and relocation. DeWitt acted quickly. First, he imposed a curfew on all alien Germans and Italians and on *all* people of Japanese ancestry who lived in one of the designated military areas. He also restricted the movement of Japanese Americans to a five-mile radius from their homes and work during non-curfew hours. Shortly thereafter, he began issuing a series of Civilian Exclusion Orders. Each of these orders designated a particular portion of the West Coast military areas from which all people of Japanese descent were excluded. They were ordered to report for evacuation from the West Coast.

authorized the secretary of war and military commanders to designate military areas from which any civilians could be excluded.

The next day, the secretary of war designated Lieutenant General John DeWitt as military commander of the Western Defense Command. DeWitt immediately issued two orders designating large parts

These exclusion orders gave Japanese American families only about a week to get ready for evacuation. They could bring merely bedrolls and such luggage as they could carry by hand. They were forced to leave their personal belongings behind, including their automobiles. Many were forced to sell their household goods and land for a pittance. Children had to leave their pets and playmates. Eventually over 120,000 Japanese Americans, two-thirds of them *citizens*, were expelled from the West Coast.

The head of the War Relocation Authority had hoped that detention of Japanese Americans in the assembly centers would be a brief stop on their way to resettlement outside the West Coast. He quickly ran into vigorous opposition from the governors and attorneys general of the western states, most of whom called for concentration camps under armed guard. The attorney general of Idaho forthrightly stated, "We want to keep this a white man's country." The War Relocation Authority caved in, and ten concentration camps were built.

Most of the Japanese went to the camps without a struggle. But that didn't mean they gave up and did not fight. Many legal suits were filed, and the cases of four internees eventually ended up before the Supreme Court. The most famous was that of Fred Korematsu.

Fred Korematsu was a twenty-two-year-old American citizen who worked as a welder in Oakland, California. He had never been out of the United States and could neither read nor write Japanese. His fiancée was Italian American. After the Pearl Harbor attack, his welder's union expelled him because of his Japanese heritage, and he consequently lost his

> While in Tanforan, Korematsu wrote a statement summarizing his opposition to internment:
>
> These camps have been definitely an imprisonment under armed guard with orders to shoot to kill. In order to be imprisoned, these people should have been given a fair trial in order that they may defend their loyalty at court in a democratic way, but they were placed in imprisonment without any fair trial. Many disloyal Germans and Italians were caught, but they were not all corralled under armed guard like the Japanese—is this a racial issue?

shipyard job. In March 1942 he had plastic surgery on his nose and eyes to alter his appearance. He feared physical attacks should people realize that he, who was planning to marry a white woman, was of Japanese ancestry. He also adopted the name of Clyde Sarah.

On May 9, instead of complying with Civilian Exclusion Order No. 34 by reporting for evacuation to the Tanforan assembly center, Korematsu remained in Oakland. He hoped to earn enough money to move to the Midwest with his fiancée.

Local police picked him up for questioning on May 30 while he was walking down the street in San Leandro, California, with his fiancée. They quickly verified his Japanese ancestry, and he was sent to Tanforan to await trial for violating the exclusion order. His fiancée broke off the engagement.

In a trial held in September 1942, Korematsu was found guilty of violating the exclusion order. He was placed on probation for five years. Although bail was posted and he should have been freed pending appeal,

Justice Hugo Black

the military police seized Korematsu while he was still in the courtroom and took him back to Tanforan.

In June 1943, in the case of *Hirabayashi v. United States*, the U.S. Supreme Court unanimously upheld the convictions of Japanese Americans who had refused to obey the curfew imposed by Lieutenant General DeWitt in March 1942. It said that the curfew was necessary to prevent sabotage and espionage, and that Japanese Americans, because of the history of discrimination against them in the United States, were likely to be loyal to Japan. Thus, racial discrimination against Japanese immigrants was used to justify further discrimination against them and their children who were citizens.

The Supreme Court acknowledged in the *Hirabayashi* case that discrimination based solely on ancestry is "odious to a free people whose institutions are founded upon the doctrine of equality." Nevertheless, the Court ruled that *no* court could review the wisdom of the actions of the government while waging war.

Chief Justice Harlan Fiske Stone wrote that although the Constitution usually prohibits the government from engaging in racial discrimination, during wartime the government was not totally prevented from treating citizens of one ancestry differently from other citizens.

Justice Frank Murphy reluctantly agreed with the *Hirabayashi* decision but wrote in a separate concurring opinion:

Under the curfew order here challenged no less than 70,000 American citizens have been placed under a special ban and deprived of their liberty because of their particular racial inheritance. In this sense it bears a melancholy resemblance to the treatment accorded to members of the Jewish race in Germany and in other parts of Europe. The result is the creation in this country of two classes of citizens for the purposes of a critical and perilous hour—to sanction discrimination between groups of United States citizens on the basis of ancestry. In my opinion this goes to the very brink of constitutional power.

Not until December 18, 1944, did the Supreme Court decide Fred Korematsu's appeal of his 1942 conviction for failing to comply with the evacuation order. Although there was absolutely no evidence of any disloyalty on Korematsu's part, he had remained incarcerated throughout his appeal. Indeed, there were no instances of sabotage or espionage by *any* Japanese Americans on the West Coast during the entire war, including the period before evacuation.

Justice Hugo Black, who had been a member of the Ku Klux Klan in Alabama from 1923 to 1926, wrote the majority opinion in the *Korematsu* case. He acknowledged that restrictions on the civil rights of a racial group are "suspect," but said "[p]ressing public necessity may sometimes justify the existence of such restrictions." He refused to acknowledge any racial prejudice in the actions taken against only one category of citizens—Japanese Americans.

Three justices dissented: Robert Jackson (later to become the chief prosecutor of Nazi war criminals at the Nuremberg Trials), Owen Roberts, and Frank Murphy.

Justice Robert Jackson wrote in his dissent:

Korematsu . . . has been convicted of

H. R. 442—2

failure of political leadership. The excluded individuals of Japanese ancestry suffered enormous damages, both material and intangible, and there were incalculable losses in education and job training, all of which resulted in significant human suffering for which appropriate compensation has not been made. For these fundamental violations of the basic civil liberties and constitutional rights of these individuals of Japanese ancestry, the Congress apologizes on behalf of the Nation.

(b) WITH RESPECT TO THE ALEUTS.—The Congress recognizes that, as described by the Commission on Wartime Relocation and Internment of Civilians, the Aleut civilian residents of the Pribilof Islands and the Aleutian Islands west of Unimak Island were relocated during World War II to temporary camps in isolated regions of southeast Alaska where they remained, under United States control and in the care of the United States, until long after any potential danger to their home villages had passed. The United States failed to provide reasonable care for the Aleuts, and this resulted in widespread illness, disease, and death among the residents of the camps; and the United States further failed to protect Aleut personal and community property while such property was in its possession or under its control. The United States has not compensated the Aleuts adequately for the conversion or destruction of personal property, and the conversion or destruction of community property caused by the United States military occupation of Aleut villages during World War II. There is no remedy for injustices suffered by the Aleuts during World War II except an Act of Congress providing appropriate compensation for those losses which are attributable to the conduct of United States forces and other officials and employees of the United States.

TITLE I—UNITED STATES CITIZENS OF JAPANESE ANCESTRY AND RESIDENT JAPANESE ALIENS

SEC 101. SHORT TITLE.
   This title may be cited as the "Civil Liberties Act of 1988".

SEC. 102. REMEDIES WITH RESPECT TO CRIMINAL CONVICTIONS.
   (a) REVIEW OF CONVICTIONS.—The Attorney General is requested to review any case in which an individual living on the date of the enactment of this Act was, while a United States citizen or permanent resident alien of Japanese ancestry, convicted of a violation of—
      (1) Executive Order Numbered 9066, dated February 19, 1942;
      (2) the Act entitled "An Act to provide a penalty for violation of restrictions or orders with respect to persons entering, remaining in, leaving, or committing any act in military areas or zones", approved March 21, 1942 (56 Stat. 173); or
      (3) any other Executive order, Presidential proclamation, law of the United States, directive of the Armed Forces of the United States, or other action taken by or on behalf of the United States or its agents, representatives, officers, or employees, respecting the evacuation, relocation, or internment of individuals solely on the basis of Japanese ancestry;

The 1988 Civil Liberties Act

an act not commonly a crime. It consists merely of being present in the state whereof he is a citizen, near the place where he was born, and where all his life he has lived. . . . [H]ere is an attempt to make an otherwise innocent act a crime merely because this prisoner is the son of parents as to whom he had no choice, and belongs to a race from which there is no way to resign.

Justice Frank Murphy began his dissent by writing, "This exclusion of 'all persons of Japanese ancestry, both alien and non-alien,' from the Pacific Coast area on a plea of military necessity in the absence of martial law ought not to be approved. Such exclusion goes over 'the very brink of constitutional power' and falls into the ugly abyss of racism." He concluded his dissent by stating, "I dissent, therefore, from this legalization of racism."

After World War II ended and people became aware of the Nazi atrocities against the Jews and others in the name of ethnic purity, attitudes slowly began to change regarding racial intolerance. In 1948, Congress passed the Japanese American

Evacuation Claims Act, which provided compensation for property losses that Japanese Americans had suffered as a result of their incarceration. Not until 1965 was the last claim paid.

In 1952, Congress repealed the racial prohibitions in the immigration and naturalization laws. However, the national origins system remained in effect, limiting the number of immigrants from specific countries. Asian countries had a quota of only two thousand per year. In the 1960s, Congress eliminated the national origins system altogether.

In 1988, Congress passed the Civil Liberties Act. It provided for additional restitution of $20,000 for the loss of civil rights for each Japanese American who had been interned. To avoid creating a precedent for Native Americans whose ancestors had been removed to make way for white expansion or for African Americans whose ancestors had been enslaved, the law limited restitution to those internees who were still living.

7

"Separate Educational Facilities Are Inherently Unequal": Is Separate Equal?

The Constitution Says . . .

"No State shall . . . deny to any person within its jurisdiction the equal protection of the laws."
—U.S. Constitution, Amendment XIV, Section 1

Pupils at a black school in Veazey, Georgia (1941)

Members of the NAACP board (1920)

On May 17, 1954, at 12:52 P.M., Chief Justice Earl Warren read the unanimous opinion of the Supreme Court decision in *Brown v. Board of Education of Topeka, Kansas.* It was the long-awaited decision that effectively overturned the *Plessy v. Ferguson* decision of 1896, the case that had institutionalized the "separate but equal" formula for maintaining segregated public schools, as well as other institutions and facilities. It was the same Constitution, but it was a different time, with different justices who had a completely different opinion. Here's how it happened:

The National Association for the Advancement of Colored People (NAACP) organized in 1909 in reaction to a race riot in Springfield, Illinois, where blacks were beaten and lynched. The purpose of the civil rights organization was to improve and protect the life and liberty of all African Americans.

In addition to legislative strategies, the NAACP pursued lawsuits in court to achieve equal rights. Instead of attacking segregation directly, however, the NAACP lawyers initially looked for cases that stressed "inequality." In the South, black schools were separate by law, but contrary to the *Plessy* "separate but equal" principle, they were almost always poorly equipped and staffed. Black administrators and teachers were paid less than their white counterparts as well. In the

Ada Lois Sipuel sought a court order from the state of Oklahoma to admit her to the state university's law school. There was no black state law school available to her. Oklahoma argued that there weren't enough blacks interested or qualified to make it worthwhile for the state to open a law school for blacks. In 1948, the Supreme Court ordered Oklahoma to provide Sipuel with a law-school education equal to what it provided for whites. In response, Oklahoma roped off a section of the state capitol building and called it a law school for colored students.

The LDF, led by Thurgood Marshall, went back to the Supreme Court, asking for an order requiring Oklahoma to admit Sipuel, arguing for the first time for an end to segregation. Legal education, Marshall argued, is collegial, and segregation brands blacks as inferior.

The Supreme Court, however, was not ready to end segregation. It ruled that it hadn't ordered Oklahoma to admit Sipuel to the white law school, only that Oklahoma could not treat her unequally. Rather than build a new law school for blacks, Oklahoma admitted Sipuel to its state law school in 1949.

The Supreme Court decision in *Sipuel v. University of Oklahoma* led the LDF to argue in other cases both that segregation should be struck down and also that black and white schools were unequal.

A 1948 photograph of (left to right) Dr. J. E. Fellows, Thurgood Marshall (standing left), Mrs. Ada Lois Sipuel Fisher, and Mr. Amos T. Hall (standing right). Thurgood Marshall was director of the Legal Defense and Education Fund from 1939 to 1961, then was appointed to the Court of Appeals for the Second Circuit in 1961 by President John F. Kennedy. In 1967, he was appointed to the Supreme Court by President Lyndon B. Johnson. Marshall was the first African American Supreme Court justice.

Linda Brown in her segregated classroom at the Monroe School, Topeka, Kansas (1953)

the "separate but equal" standard would result in the end of segregation because it would be too expensive for states to maintain two equal school systems.

In the 1940s, the Legal Defense and Education Fund (LDF), the legal arm of the NAACP, filed cases to get "separate but equal" legally enforced in schools. But by the end of the 1940s, the LDF decided to attack segregation directly.

It filed the first public-school desegregation case in 1950, *Briggs v. Elliott*, which challenged Clarendon County, South Carolina's segregated school system. A panel of three federal district court judges in South Carolina heard the case and ruled only that the schools had to be equalized. This decision upheld segregation because it did not question the legality of separate facilities.

Undaunted, the LDF, led by Thurgood Marshall, filed *Brown v. Board of Education of Topeka, Kansas*, in 1951 on behalf of twenty plaintiffs. The case was named after the first plaintiff, Linda Brown, a black child in Topeka, whose father, Oliver Brown, was a welder on the Santa Fe Railroad. Her father had tried to register his third-grade daughter in an all-white school because, like the other black children in her neighborhood, Linda Brown

early 1900s, $15.41 a year was spent on education for every white child. Only $1.50 was spent on each African American student. By the 1930s, as many as 230 Southern counties had no black high schools. And after World War II, the capital outlay for black schools was 23 percent of outlays for Southern white schools. Some states had no professional or graduate schools for blacks to attend. Students had to leave their state to get a law, medical, or postgraduate degree.

The NAACP thought that demanding equal schools for blacks and whites using

Not only did the LDF lose the trial, but there were devastating ramifications for blacks in Clarendon County. Many of the county's black political and educational leaders were fired from their jobs, denied credit, refused renewal of leases, sued for slander, forced to pay off debts early, and threatened by the Klan. In one case, a black person was beaten to death.

Chief Justice Earl Warren (1948)

courts, to resolve. To get around the *Plessy* standard of "equality," the states argued that black and white schools were equal already or were in the process of being equalized.

The case was heard by the Supreme Court twice, first in December 1952. The High Court was divided after the first argument. A second oral argument was scheduled, but before it could begin, Chief Justice Fred M. Vinson died unexpectedly. President Dwight D. Eisenhower appointed Earl Warren as chief justice in the fall of 1953. The reargument took place in December 1953 and lasted three days. Chief Justice Warren delayed the Court's ruling until he could get a unanimous decision on *Brown*. He argued that a unanimous opinion was essential if the Court was to persuade the nation that segregation was unconstitutional.

Once this was achieved, Chief Justice Warren wrote the unanimous decision of the Court. He wrote a short and easy-to-

was bused to a black school miles from her home. Instead of arguing that Brown's all-black school was inferior, Marshall attacked segregation directly. He and his legal team presented powerful evidence that segregation had a negative psychological impact on black children.

By the time the Supreme Court took the case in 1952, there were five cases before the Court challenging segregation, including *Briggs v. Elliot*. The Court consolidated all the cases for hearing.

The briefs filed by states supporting segregation basically relied on states' rights. The states argued that segregation was a matter for state legislatures, not the

Southern politicians argued that the Supreme Court was interfering in a state matter. In an angry response, South Carolina and several other states began flying the rebel (Confederate) flag, which had not been flown in the South since the Civil War, over the state capitol and other state buildings as a symbol of their defiance. To civil rights supporters and especially African Americans, the flag became a symbol of the state's disregard for civil and often human rights. During the late 1990s, when a multiracial coalition demanded that the Confederate flag be removed from Georgia's and South Carolina's capitols, some Americans did not understand why. These states had begun flying the Confederate flag in the 1950s as a symbol of their defiance of segregation. It was not just to honor Civil War veterans.

understand opinion, one that could be easily reproduced for people to read in the mass media. He concluded that it was impossible to determine what the framers of the Fourteenth Amendment intended as to segregated schools. The Court therefore decided to focus on public education as it existed in the 1950s, when it heard the case, to determine if school segregation violated the Equal Protection Clause of the Fourteenth Amendment. The justices concluded that it did.

Chief Justice Warren quoted from the Kansas trial court's findings as to the effect segregation has on black children:

> Segregation of white and colored children in public schools has a detrimental effect upon the colored children. The impact is greater when it has the sanction of the law, for the policy of separating the races is usually interpreted as denoting the inferiority of the negro group. A sense of inferiority affects the motivation of a child to learn. Segregation with the sanction of law, therefore, has a tendency to [retard] the educational and mental development of negro children and to deprive them of some of the benefits they would receive in a racially integrated school system.

Although the Court did not explicitly overrule the 1896 *Plessy* decision, it strongly undermined *Plessy* by stating that "in the field of public education the doctrine of 'separate but equal' has no place. Separate educational facilities are inherently unequal." Another Supreme Court decision, concerning the Montgomery bus boycott, officially overturned the *Plessy* decision in 1956.

Reaction to the *Brown* decision ranged from elation to outrage. After *Brown*, some school districts in Missouri, Kansas, Indiana, and parts of West Virginia and Maryland quietly integrated. Although a few superintendents, principals, and teachers resigned rather than integrate, there were just as many educators who willingly accepted the challenge with enthusiasm. Resistance in the Deep South, however, impeded all movement toward the implementation of *Brown*. Over 80 percent of Southern whites opposed *Brown*. Some politicians were openly discussing secession.

But opposition to *Brown* was not limited to the South. The LDF returned to the Supreme Court to get an order against the board of education of Topeka, Kansas, for immediate integration, but the High Court refused. Instead, it issued an ambiguous ruling that the schools were to desegregate with "all deliberate speed." Those who opposed the original ruling saw a loophole

Throughout the South, laws were passed that required NAACP membership lists to be disclosed to state authorities. Alabama passed a law banning the NAACP. Virginia passed a law designed to prevent the NAACP from preparing lawsuits. Three times the Supreme Court heard cases challenging these attacks on the NAACP. In 1958, 1963, and 1964, the Supreme Court struck down these laws. Nevertheless, the attacks on the NAACP took their toll. Members were harassed at their jobs and even fired. Some states made it illegal for teachers or state employees to belong to the NAACP or be involved in the practice of "race mixing." From 1955 to 1958, the NAACP lost 246 branches throughout the South, but people continued to support its efforts anonymously.

Hooded Ku Klux Klansmen burning a cross in protest of racial integration in Tallulah, Louisiana (1962)

that would allow them to stall the process indefinitely. President Eisenhower declined to endorse the *Brown* decision, saying that he would not approve or disapprove of it. Then he publicly denounced his appointment of Chief Justice Earl Warren, saying that it was "the biggest . . . fool mistake I ever made." Clearly the moral imperative of *Brown* had been weakened.

The reaction of those vehemently opposed to school desegregation seemed to be: The Supreme Court has made its ruling; now let it enforce it! With the philosophy, "If we can legislate, we can segregate," states passed 450 laws to keep public schools segregated.

In some areas, authorities approved plans that integrated one grade at a time. In others, they postponed complying with the *Brown* decision by filing endless lawsuits and by economic intimidation, even by shutting down schools. One popular form of resistance was freedom-of-choice plans that allowed parents to choose all-white schools for their children. Another was pupil-placement laws that gave local authorities power to accept or reject pupils requesting admission to particular schools. Private and church-sponsored white-only schools multiplied rapidly, and homeschooling became still another option.

In the meantime, Klan activities such as public marches and recruitment meetings increased as a way to frighten those who might support school desegregation. When all else failed, Southern politicians openly and defiantly disobeyed court orders to desegregate.

But a Little Rock, Arkansas, incident finally forced President Eisenhower to take a stand. Arkansas was not considered a Deep South state. However, in 1956, Governor Orval Faubus capitalized on racism, fear, and ignorance to garner votes in his successful reelection campaign. He promised never to allow integration in the state of Arkansas.

Nine African American high school students were scheduled to enroll at the all-white Central High School in Little Rock on September 3, 1957. The school board's decision to integrate had not met with much resistance. The high school administration and faculty had not anticipated any problems. But the night before the school was to open, Governor Faubus declared the school off-limits for black students. He appeared on a local television station and announced that he would not be responsible for the violence that was bound to happen if black students tried to attend the school. He also dispatched the Arkansas National Guard to Central High School. The school board, which had not requested the governor's intervention, asked black students not to attend school until the courts could resolve the matter.

On September 3, the district court ordered the school board to proceed with the integration. The next day, when the black students showed up at school, the Arkansas National Guard forcibly prevented them from entering. It continued to do so until September 20, when the district court issued an injunction ordering the governor and national guard to stop preventing black students from attending

Central High School. When the students went to school on Monday, September 23, an unruly mob gathered and made it worse.

On September 24, President Eisenhower took control of the national guard from state governors, and one thousand troops were dispatched from the 101st Airborne

67

Richard Richardson, 17, and Harold Smith, 17, attempting to enter North Little Rock High School (September 9, 1957)

Division out of Kentucky. The next morning, paratroopers—some of whom were black—escorted the nine students into Central High School. Throughout the rest of the school year, army troops or national guardsmen remained on duty at Central High to enforce the rights of black students to attend school.

Eisenhower explained in an address to the nation that he was not using troops to defend integration but to uphold national supremacy, defend presidential authority, and enforce the law of the land as stated by the Supreme Court.

Although by 1958 over 300,000 black children were attending desegregated schools, 2.4 million were still in segregated situations.

Because of the persistent resistance to the *Brown* decision, case after case landed in court, with the plaintiffs seeking court orders to force school districts to desegregate. Judges had to devise ways to eliminate segregation whenever school districts refused to eliminate it themselves. The judges' jobs were made more difficult due to noncooperation by hostile school districts.

Faced with years of resistance and con-

Supreme Court of the United States

No. 1 ——— , *October Term, 19* 54

Oliver Brown, Mrs. Richard Lawton, Mrs. Sadie Emmanuel et al.,
Appellants,

vs.

Board of Education of Topeka, Shawnee County, Kansas, et al.

Appeal from *the United States District Court for the* ———————— *District of Kansas.*

This cause *came on to be heard on the transcript of the record from the United States District Court for the* ———————— *District of Kansas,* ———————— *and was argued by counsel.*

On consideration whereof, *It is ordered and adjudged by this Court that the judgment of the said* District ———————— *Court in this cause be, and the same is* hereby, reversed *with costs; and that this cause be, and the same is* remanded *to the said District Court to take such* proceedings and enter such orders and decrees consistent with the opinions of this Court as are necessary and proper to admit to public schools on a racially nondiscriminatory basis with all deliberate speed the parties to this case.

Per Mr. Chief Justice Warren,
May 31, 1955.

The *Brown v. Board of Education* "All deliberate speed" ruling (1954)

tinued segregation, in 1971, the Supreme Court used the lawsuit of *Swann v. Charlotte-Mecklenburg Board of Education* to give some general guidelines as to what courts could do to eliminate segregation. The district court in North Carolina had ordered the school board to come up with a desegregation plan and, among other things, instructed the board to consider using bus transportation to accomplish desegregation. Busing was not a new concept. School systems had used busing for years to take students to schools that were not close to their homes to achieve segregation.

However, now the state of North Carolina passed its Anti-Busing Law. It prohibited busing of students based on race or for the purpose of achieving racial balance in the schools. Busing for any other reason was still permitted.

When the case reached the Supreme Court, one of the issues before the Court was whether busing could be used to help achieve integration. The Supreme Court, in two unanimous opinions written by Chief Justice Warren Burger, noted that 39 percent of all schoolchildren in the

United States were bused to school, and that busing was considered a normal tool of educational policy. Chief Justice Burger also noted that the students bused for desegregation purposes in the *Charlotte-Mecklenburg* case would be bused, on average, a far shorter distance than the almost 24,000 students already being bused by the system. The Court struck down the Anti-Busing Law, stating that enforcement of the law would:

> render illusory the promise of *Brown v. Board of Education*. Just as the race of students must be considered in determining whether a constitutional violation has occurred, so also must race be considered in formulating a remedy. To forbid, at this stage, all assignments made on the basis of race would deprive school authorities of the one tool absolutely essential to fulfillment of their constitutional obligation to eliminate existing dual [i.e., segregated] school systems.

White opposition to busing resulted in violent protests from Boston to Richmond and from Dallas to Cleveland. Even today, school desegregation and how to achieve it remains one of the most hotly debated issues in education, and courts continue to wrestle with it. In each of the past twelve years, segregation in schools has *increased*. Thus, grade schools and high schools are actually *resegregating*.

In 1954, *Brown v. Board of Education* leveled a stunning blow against segregation, but it by no means ended it or the need for civil rights legislation.

The first civil rights bill to be adopted since Reconstruction was passed in 1957 and signed by President Eisenhower. Its most significant provision was the creation of a nonpartisan federal civil rights commission to study the status of civil rights in the nation and make recommendations for legislation.

It did not have the depth and scope the NAACP had hoped for, but it was a beginning. The Civil Rights Act of 1957 opened the door for stronger and more effective civil rights legislation in the 1960s.

"To Banish the Blight of Racial Discrimination": Enforcing Equality

The Constitution Says . . .
"The Congress shall have Power . . . to regulate Commerce . . . among the several States. . . ."
—U.S. Constitution, Article I, Section 8, Clause 3

"Neither slavery nor involuntary servitude, except as a punishment for crime whereof the party shall have been duly convicted, shall exist within the United States, or any place subject to their jurisdiction."
—U.S. Constitution, Amendment XIII, Section 1

"Congress shall have power to enforce this article by appropriate legislation."
—U.S. Constitution, Amendment XIII, Section 2

"The right of citizens of the United States to vote shall not be denied or abridged by the United States or by any State on account of race, color, or previous condition of servitude."
—U.S. Constitution, Amendment XV, Section 1

"Congress shall have the power to enforce this article by appropriate legislation."
—U.S. Constitution, Amendment XV, Section 2

8

Overturning the *Plessy* decision was one thing. Dismantling segregation and enforcing civil rights was another.

In 1960, John F. Kennedy won the presidency by a narrow margin over Vice President Richard M. Nixon. Civil rights were not a priority of the Kennedy administration at first. In fact, several of President Kennedy's judicial appointees to the federal bench were arch-segregationists.

By 1963, however, as the civil rights movement grew stronger, President Kennedy had come full circle and was ready to use his executive power in the struggle for justice and equality. He asked Congress to draft legislation that would ban segregation in public facilities, broaden the powers of the Justice Department to enforce school integration, and extend federal protection of voting rights.

In August 1963, over 250,000 Americans from all over the country gathered in Washington, D.C., to urge Congress to pass the proposed civil rights legislation. The speakers asked for equal rights as guaranteed to all U.S. citizens, as well as fair employment. The speech most remembered that day was made by the Reverend Dr. Martin Luther King Jr., whose "I Have a Dream" address captured the essence of the struggle in a few elegant words.

The 1963 March on Washington inspired others to join the movement, if no more than to send a donation. Now millions of men and women of all races and religions were united in the demand for freedom, justice, and equality. In September, when a bomb exploded in a Birmingham, Alabama, church, tragically

The Reverend Dr. Martin Luther King Jr. delivers his "I Have a Dream" speech during the March on Washington (August 28, 1963).

taking the lives of four young Sunday-school children, people were horrified at the cowardly violence. Still, the marchers and protesters refused to back down.

Though the country was shocked by the assassination of President John F. Kennedy on November 22, 1963, the new president, Lyndon B. Johnson, was determined to move ahead with many of Kennedy's plans, including the civil rights bill. He got the bill passed by June 1964 and signed it into law on July 2.

The 1964 Civil Rights Act was the most comprehensive civil rights legislation ever enacted by Congress. The law included several sections or "titles" that contained many provisions designed to end discrimination.

These measures not only allowed individuals to sue when they were victims of discrimination but also gave the attorney general of the United States the power, in some circumstances, to sue those who continued to practice discrimination or segregation in public accommodations, to enforce school desegregation, and to sue those engaging in a pattern of employment discrimination.

As soon as the Civil Rights Act was passed, a segregationist motel owner in Atlanta, Georgia, filed suit to prevent

72

enforcement of the law. He refused to rent rooms to African Americans. His motel, which had 216 units, was located close to downtown Atlanta. He advertised his hotel in national magazines; about 75 percent of his customers were from out of state. The motel owner claimed that he had a right to continue to exclude blacks from his motel because he was a private citizen and not an agent of the state. He argued that the Civil Rights Act violated the Constitution.

Congress based its authority to pass the civil rights bill on the Equal Protection Clause of the Fourteenth Amendment, as well as its power to regulate interstate commerce under Article I of the Constitution. In 1883, the Supreme Court had ruled that Congress had no authority under the Fourteenth Amendment to pass a national civil rights law because that

Justice Tom C. Clark (1950s)

amendment only prohibited *states*—not individuals—from denying equal rights.

In 1964, by contrast, the Supreme Court ruled unanimously in *Heart of Atlanta Motel v. U.S.*, in an opinion written by Justice Tom C. Clark, that the 1964 Civil Rights Act was constitutional. The Court avoided making any decision about Congress's power under the Fourteenth Amendment's Equal Protection Clause. Instead, the Court focused on the broad reach of the Commerce Clause of the Constitution, which provides, "The Congress shall have Power . . . to regulate Commerce . . . among the several States. . . ."

In the *Heart of Atlanta Motel* case, the Supreme Court concluded that the Commerce Clause gave Congress the power to pass a national civil rights law and quoted from Chief Justice Marshall's 1824 *Gibbons v. Ogden* decision, which gave the federal government power to regulate commerce that affected more than one state.

The Court concluded that the motel had an effect on interstate commerce, even though it was located only in Georgia. Why? Because African American travelers, many of whom were traveling from one state to another (in other words, interstate), had difficulty finding lodging because of the racial discrimination practiced by the Heart of Atlanta Motel (and most other hotels and motels in the South).

Justice Clark concluded the opinion with a resounding reaffirmation of Congress's power under the Commerce Clause:

> We, therefore, conclude that the action of the Congress in the adoption of the Act as applied here to a motel which concededly serves interstate travelers is within the power granted it by the Commerce Clause of the Constitution, as interpreted by this Court for 140 years. It may be argued that Congress could have pursued other methods to eliminate the obstructions it found in interstate commerce caused by racial discrimination. But this is a matter of policy that rests entirely with the Congress not with the courts.

So ended the argument that individuals could discriminate against a person with impunity. The *Heart of Atlanta Motel* deci-

sion also meant that Congress could prohibit employment discrimination.

Before passage of the 1964 Civil Rights Act, private employers throughout the United States could discriminate against job applicants or employees based on their race, national origin, sex, religion, age, disability, or sexual orientation. Employees had no legal recourse unless they lived in a state that had its own civil rights law. Title VII of the Civil Rights Act changed that in part. It prohibited job discrimination based on race, sex, religion, and national origin, but it did not prohibit other types of job discrimination.

Although desegregation of public accommodations occurred rapidly after the passage of the 1964 Civil Rights Act and the *Heart of Atlanta Motel* decision, employment discrimination remained pervasive. The Equal Employment Opportunity Commission (EEOC), established by Title VII of the Civil Rights Act to enforce the law, was overwhelmed with complaints. Many of those facing job discrimination were forced to file lawsuits, which often took years to resolve. To this day, the EEOC has an enormous backlog.

At the same time Congress was debating the Civil Rights Act of 1964, white and black students were working to register African American voters throughout the South.

In the 1890s, Southern states had begun using various tactics to disenfranchise blacks: poll taxes, literacy tests, property and "good character" qualifications, and requirements that voters be able to understand or interpret the law.

Literacy tests, in theory, sounded reasonable. But the questions used to test literacy were *not* reasonable. Sometimes citizens had to recite the entire federal and state constitutions from memory. Citizens were asked to answer ridiculous questions, such as "How high is up?" or "How many angels can dance on the head of a pin?" People who had earned college degrees were declared unqualified to vote because they could not pass these kinds of literacy tests. After a while, a majority of blacks gave up and didn't even try to register to vote.

Before the 1960s, the Supreme Court had upheld many of these states' actions, ruling that it was the states' right to set voter-registration criteria. The Civil Rights Acts of 1957, 1960, and 1964 broadened the power of the federal attorney general and courts to attack voting rights violations, yet progress continued at a snail's pace.

In Dallas County, Alabama, where Selma is the county seat, four years of litigation by the Justice Department resulted in black voter registration increasing only from 156 to 383, although there were about 15,000 voting-age blacks in the county. To emphasize the need for better legislation, Martin Luther King Jr. and other civil rights leaders organized a march from Selma to Montgomery. Governor George Wallace warned them not to proceed with their plans. The march took place on March 7, 1965, in spite of the threats. State troopers attacked the marchers, who were not resisting, with cattle prods and whips. The nation watched in horror as law enforcement officers beat peaceful demonstrators.

Meanwhile, a federal judge overruled Governor Wallace and permitted the Selma to Montgomery march to take place. Americans from all over the country converged on Selma for a second march on March 21. President Johnson gave his support by sending federal troops. With 2,200 troops protecting 25,000 demonstrators along the eighty-mile walk, there was very little Wallace could do but watch.

On March 15, 1965, President Lyndon Johnson spoke to a joint session of Congress and asked for a strong voting rights bill. On August 6, 1965, Congress passed the Voting Rights Act.

Although the Voting Rights Act didn't apply to all states, it was a major civil rights victory. The act applied to those states that used literacy tests, and where less than 50 percent of adults were registered to vote. The law was directed primarily at those Southern states that were most reprehensible in disenfranchising blacks. It didn't affect Arkansas, Texas, and Florida, which didn't use literacy tests.

The key provisions of the act included:

- no abridgment of the right to vote on the basis of race
- no literacy tests for five years
- no new voting regulations without approval
- the U.S. attorney general could send federal examiners and poll watchers to the states in question.

In 1966, the Supreme Court upheld the constitutionality of the act in the case of

South Carolina v. Katzenbach. Chief Justice Earl Warren wrote in the eight-to-one decision that the 1965 Voting Rights Act was passed "to banish the blight of racial discrimination in voting." He held that "Congress may use any rational means to effectuate the constitutional prohibition of racial discrimination in voting."

The Voting Rights Act had an immediate impact on black voter registration because the Justice Department sent federal examiners to the most recalcitrant counties in four states. By 1968, black voter registration had jumped to 60 percent in Mississippi and to 57 percent in Alabama. In the South as a whole, black voter registration increased to 62 percent as a million blacks were registered to vote for the first time. Blacks began competing for elective positions formerly held only by whites—such as mayors, sheriffs, prosecuting attorneys, governors, and state and federal representatives.

The Voting Rights Act would have expired in 1982, but Congress extended it for another twenty-five years. It will expire

MISSING CALL FBI

THE FBI IS SEEKING INFORMATION CONCERNING THE DISAPPEARANCE AT PHILADELPHIA, MISSISSIPPI, OF THESE THREE INDIVIDUALS ON JUNE 21, 1964. EXTENSIVE INVESTIGATION IS BEING CONDUCTED TO LOCATE GOODMAN, CHANEY, AND SCHWERNER, WHO ARE DESCRIBED AS FOLLOWS:

ANDREW GOODMAN   JAMES EARL CHANEY   MICHAEL HENRY SCHWERNER

RACE:	White	Negro	White
SEX:	Male	Male	Male
DOB:	November 23, 1943	May 30, 1943	November 6, 1939
POB:	New York City	Meridian, Mississippi	New York City
AGE:	20 years	21 years	24 years
HEIGHT:	5'10"	5'7"	5'9" to 5'10"
WEIGHT:	150 pounds	135 to 140 pounds	170 to 180 pounds
HAIR:	Dark brown; wavy	Black	Brown
EYES:	Brown	Brown	Light blue
TEETH:		Good: none missing	
SCARS AND MARKS:		1 inch cut scar 2 inches above left ear.	Pock mark center of forehead, slight scar on bridge of nose, appendectomy scar, broken leg scar.

SHOULD YOU HAVE OR IN THE FUTURE RECEIVE ANY INFORMATION CONCERNING THE WHEREABOUTS OF THESE INDIVIDUALS, YOU ARE REQUESTED TO NOTIFY ME OR THE NEAREST OFFICE OF THE FBI. TELEPHONE NUMBER IS LISTED BELOW.

June 29, 1964

DIRECTOR
FEDERAL BUREAU OF INVESTIGATION
UNITED STATES DEPARTMENT OF JUSTICE
WASHINGTON, D. C. 20535
TELEPHONE, NATIONAL 8-7117

After decades of being disenfranchised, blacks began to reassert their right to vote by participating in massive voter-registration drives, beginning in the 1960s. The feelings were, if blacks could vote, they would elect people who represented them and their interests. In June 1964, two white civil rights workers, Andrew Goodman and Michael Schwerner, traveled to Mississippi to help with the movement. James Chaney, who lived in Philadelphia, Mississippi, showed them around. Just outside the town, their car was pulled over by Deputy Sheriff Cecil Price, who released them to a group of Klansmen. The three young men were never seen alive again. Their bodies were found in August in a mud dam in the Tallahala Creek, where the Klansmen had buried them.

in 2007 unless Congress renews it again.

The 1964 Civil Rights Act had not dealt with the widespread problem of housing

WILDER

VOTE DEC. 2 **VOTE DEC. 2**

FOR

STATE SENATE

YOU CAN MAKE DEMOCRACY WORK!

Although Douglas Wilder (above) was elected governor of Virginia in 1989, to date no African American senator has been elected from a Southern state since Reconstruction. Edward Brooke of Massachusetts (right) and Carol Moseley Braun of Illinois have served in the U.S. Senate.

ATTORNEY   VETERAN
EDWARD WILLIAM

BROOKE

For

REPRESENTATIVE
WARD 12

segregation and discrimination. It was easier for Congress to think of discrimination and segregation as a Southern problem. Yet housing segregation was prevalent throughout the North. As blacks moved from the South to the urban North during and after World War I, the National Association of Real Estate Boards pro-

duced a so-called code of ethics that *required* its members to help maintain segregated neighborhoods. Banks often refused to lend money to either minorities or whites to buy homes in minority neighborhoods. Some white neighborhoods established "restrictive covenants," which homeowners signed, agreeing not to sell to minorities.

The federal government likewise promoted racial segregation. The Federal Housing Administration insured home mortgages in white suburbs while often refusing to insure mortgages in the inner cities, where blacks tended to live. Federal housing projects were segregated. Urban renewal projects, which were promoted as slum clearance, often became excuses to displace blacks from their homes.

In St. Louis County, Missouri, Joseph Lee Jones and his wife, Barbara Jo, attempted to buy a home but were turned down. The Joneses believed that they were denied the opportunity because Mr. Jones was African American. They wanted to sue the real-estate agent for race discrimination.

The Joneses' attorney, Samuel Liberman of St. Louis, searched the statute books to find a law he could use to sue the real-estate agent. He came across an 1866 federal civil rights law that was reenacted in 1870, after passage of the Fourteenth Amendment. The statute provided: "All citizens of the United States shall have the same right in every State and Territory as is enjoyed by white citizens thereof to inherit, purchase, lease, sell, hold, and convey real and personal property."

The Joneses filed suit against the real-estate agent in the case of *Jones v. Alfred H. Mayer Co.* Although the statute had been on the books for one hundred years, it had rarely been used to challenge racial discrimination. A key issue that the Supreme Court had to decide was whether Congress had had the authority to pass this civil rights law.

In 1968, the Court ruled seven to two that Section 2 of the Thirteenth Amendment, which gives Congress the power to enforce the prohibition against slavery "by appropriate legislation," means that Congress has the power to outlaw all racial barriers to buying property. Justice Potter Stewart wrote in his opinion for the Court that the Thirteenth Amendment gives Congress the "power to pass all laws necessary and proper for abolishing all badges and incidents of slavery in the United States."

While the *Jones* case was pending,

H. R. 2516—9

(1) have the document entitled "Indian Affairs, Laws and Treaties" (Senate Document Numbered 319, volumes 1 and 2, Fifty-eighth Congress), revised and extended to include all treaties, laws, Executive orders, and regulations relating to Indian affairs in force on September 1, 1967, and to have such revised document printed at the Government Printing Office;
(2) have revised and republished the treatise entitled "Federal Indian Law"; and
(3) have prepared, to the extent determined by the Secretary of the Interior to be feasible, an accurate compilation of the official opinions, published and unpublished, of the Solicitor of the Department of the Interior relating to Indian affairs rendered by the Solicitor prior to September 1, 1967, and to have such compilation printed as a Government publication at the Government Printing Office.
(b) With respect to the document entitled "Indian Affairs, Laws and Treaties" as revised and extended in accordance with paragraph (1) of subsection (a), and the compilation prepared in accordance with paragraph (3) of such subsection, the Secretary of the Interior shall take such action as may be necessary to keep such document and compilation current on an annual basis.
(c) There is authorized to be appropriated for carrying out the provisions of this title, with respect to the preparation but not including printing, such sum as may be necessary.

TITLE VIII—FAIR HOUSING

POLICY

SEC. 801. It is the policy of the United States to provide, within constitutional limitations, for fair housing throughout the United States.

DEFINITIONS

SEC. 802. As used in this title—
(a) "Secretary" means the Secretary of Housing and Urban Development.
(b) "Dwelling" means any building, structure, or portion thereof which is occupied as, or designed or intended for occupancy as, a residence by one or more families, and any vacant land which is offered for sale or lease for the construction or location thereon of any such building, structure, or portion thereof.
(c) "Family" includes a single individual.
(d) "Person" includes one or more individuals, corporations, partnerships, associations, labor organizations, legal representatives, mutual companies, joint-stock companies, trusts, unincorporated organizations, trustees, trustees in bankruptcy, receivers, and fiduciaries.
(e) "To rent" includes to lease, to sublease, to let and otherwise to grant for a consideration the right to occupy premises not owned by the occupant.
(f) "Discriminatory housing practice" means an act that is unlawful under section 804, 805, or 806.
(g) "State" means any of the several States, the District of Columbia, the Commonwealth of Puerto Rico, or any of the territories and possessions of the United States.

The Fair Housing Act of 1968

Congress began debating a fair housing bill. As the civil rights movement moved north after the 1964 Civil Rights Act and the 1965 Voting Rights Act, one of the key demands was for an end to housing discrimination. The assassination of Martin Luther King Jr. on April 4, 1968, and the resulting urban revolts propelled Congress, at last, to pass a housing rights law, the Fair Housing Act of 1968. The act outlawed discrimination on the basis of race, color, religion, or national origin in virtually all housing and mortgage transactions.

Between 1964 and 1968, the Supreme Court issued three landmark decisions upholding congressional power to pass civil rights laws. These decisions paved the way for women to seek their rights in court as well.

"Separate and Unequal": Should a Citizen's Gender Affect the Constitutional Interpretation of the Law?

The Constitution Says . . .
"No State shall . . . deny to any person . . . the equal protection of the laws."
—U.S. Constitution, Amendment XIV, Section 1

Proposed Equal Rights Amendment to U.S. Constitution, never ratified:
"Equality of rights under the law shall not be denied or abridged by the United States or any State on account of sex."

9

Officers of the National Women's Party in front of their Washington headquarters holding a banner with a Susan B. Anthony quote (1920s)

The Nineteenth Amendment gave women the right to vote, but it did not ensure equal rights in employment and education. The women's movement that had led the fight for ratification of the suffrage amendment split over the question of equal rights for women.

One branch of the women's movement was led by the National Women's Party (NWP), which believed in complete equality of the sexes. Passage of an amendment to give equal rights to women became the primary goal of the NWP for the next half century. In 1943, the NWP reworded the proposed amendment to read: "Equality of rights under the law shall not be denied or abridged by the United States or any State on account of sex." Those who supported the Equal Rights Amendment (ERA) tended to be business and professional women, Republican women, and conservative Southern Democratic women.

The other branch of the women's movement became the League of Women Voters. Although the league worked to overturn specific laws that discriminated against women, it opposed the ERA, fearing it would invalidate protective labor laws, which it supported. Protective labor laws limited the number of hours that women could work but also included those that improved working conditions specifically for women. Labor unions supported these laws, hoping that improving working conditions for women would eventually lead to better conditions for all workers. The National Women's Party opposed protective labor laws. They viewed such laws as furthering discrimination against women.

Supporters of the ERA had been successful in getting the Republican Party in 1940 and the Democratic Party in 1944 to support the ERA in their platforms. But the effort to pass the ERA at that time failed due to opposition from many liberal organizations.

The Supreme Court, meanwhile, refused to interpret the Fourteenth Amendment's Equal Protection Clause as prohibiting states from discriminating against women. The labor movement's drive to protect women from certain working conditions had led to restrictions or complete exclusion from various occupations. Michigan, for example, passed a law that a woman could not work as a bartender unless she was the wife or daughter of a male owner. The Supreme Court upheld this law in 1948 in *Goesaert v. Cleary*, ruling that it did not violate the Fourteenth Amendment's Equal Protection Clause. Then, in 1961, the Supreme Court unanimously upheld a Florida law that exempted women (but not men) from jury service

Justice Felix Frankfurter wrote for the majority in *Goesaert v. Cleary*:

Since bartending by women may . . . give rise to moral and social problems against which [the legislature] may devise preventive measures, the legislature need not go to the full length of prohibition if it believes that as to a defined group of females other factors are operating which either eliminate or reduce the moral and social problems otherwise calling for prohibition. Michigan evidently believes that the oversight assured through ownership of a bar by a barmaid's husband or father minimizes the hazards that may confront a barmaid without such protecting oversight.

Justice John Marshall Harlan, grandson of the first Justice Harlan, wrote in the 1961 *Hoyt v. Florida* decision:

Despite the enlightened emancipation of women from the restrictions and protections of bygone years, and their entry into many parts of community life formerly considered to be reserved to men, woman is still regarded as the center of home and family life. We cannot say that it is constitutionally impermissible for a State, acting in pursuit of the general welfare, to conclude that a woman should be relieved from the civic duty of jury service unless she herself determines that such service is consistent with her own special responsibilities.

unless they voluntarily registered.

Despite the 1948 and 1961 Supreme Court decisions, President John F. Kennedy's Commission on the Status of Women concluded in its 1963 report that the ERA was not necessary because women had protection from discrimination under the Fourteenth Amendment. Nevertheless, in 1963, Congress passed the Equal Pay Act, mandating equal pay for equal work, and President Kennedy signed the bill.

When the historic 1964 Civil Rights Act was being debated, the National Women's Party convinced Representative Howard Smith of Virginia to add "sex" to race, religion, and national origin in the protections from discrimination in employment. The NWP stated in its 1963 resolution in support of this amendment that otherwise, the bill would not give "a White woman, a Woman of the Christian Religion, or a Woman of United States Origin the protection it would afford to Negroes." The lead-

ership of the Southern Democratic Congressmen overwhelmingly supported the addition of "sex" to the Civil Rights Act, in hopes of killing the bill. Congresswomen also supported the addition of "sex" to the bill but on different grounds—that women were entitled to equal rights. By a vote of 168 to 133, the House voted to approve Representative Smith's amendment. The House then voted to pass the entire Civil Rights Act, including the amendment that prohibited discrimination based on sex. Thus, the Southern strategy to defeat the bill by adding "sex" to the protected categories failed. A Southerner, President Lyndon B. Johnson, signed the bill into law.

Within a few years of passage of the 1964 Civil Rights Act, the Equal Employment Opportunity Commission began ruling that protective labor laws violated the Civil Rights Act.

Gradually a new women's rights movement emerged, beginning in the late 1960s. The African American civil rights movement and the antiwar movement invigorated it. Both groups had organized widespread opposition to the Vietnam War. Women began questioning and challenging sex roles in the family, in the workplace, and throughout society. The women's movement affected both Congress and the Supreme Court.

The drive to pass the ERA, which had been dormant for a generation, came to life again. After he took office in 1969, President Richard M. Nixon appointed the President's Task Force on Women's Rights and Responsibilities. That task force recommended that Congress pass the ERA and send it to the states for ratification.

In 1970, 72 senators and 223 representatives cosponsored the ERA in Congress. The ERA touched off a furious congressional debate over the role of women. Senator Samuel Ervin Jr. of North Carolina, who had opposed all civil rights bills and had signed the Southern Manifesto against the *Brown v. Board of Education* decision, led the fight in the Senate against the ERA. He opposed the concept of equality and argued that the ERA would eliminate legal distinctions between men and women and would undermine the traditional role of women. He also opposed giving the federal courts power to interpret the ERA to determine if state laws complied with it.

While the ERA was being debated in Congress, the Supreme Court, for the first time ever, struck down a sex-discriminatory law on the grounds that it violated the Fourteenth Amendment's Equal Protection Clause. The case involved a dispute between the parents of Richard Lynn Reed, a boy who died in Idaho in 1967 with a small estate (less than $1,000 in value). Although so little money was involved, his estate had to go through a probate court. His mother, Sally Reed, asked the court to appoint her as the administrator who would handle her son's estate. Richard's father, Cecil Reed, filed a competing petition asking the court to appoint him. The probate court said both parents were equally qualified to be appointed. However, relying on an Idaho law that gave preference to males over females as administrators, the court appointed the father to handle his son's estate. Sally Reed

appealed; the Idaho appeals court ruled that the law violated the Equal Protection Clause. The father appealed to the Idaho Supreme Court, which reversed the decision of the appeals court, ruling that the law did not violate the Equal Protection Clause. Sally Reed asked the U.S. Supreme Court to hear the case.

The Court unanimously ruled in *Reed v. Reed* in 1971 that the Idaho law that gave preference to men over women in appointing people to handle the estate of a deceased person was unconstitutional. Chief Justice Warren Burger wrote: "To give a mandatory preference to members of either sex over members of the other . . . is to make the very kind of arbitrary legislative choice forbidden by the Equal Protection Clause of the Fourteenth Amendment."

The decision of the Court did not even mention the Court's 1961 jury-service decision (also unanimous) that had upheld different treatment of men and women. In just one decade, the Supreme Court did an about-face on the question of the Equal Protection Clause and sex discrimination.

Meanwhile, the ERA passed Congress in 1972 by a vote of 354 to 23 in the House and 84 to 8 in the Senate, and was sent to the states for ratification. With the overwhelming vote for the ERA by Congress, ratification seemed assured. By 1975, thirty-four of the thirty-eight states necessary for ratification had voted to ratify.

At the same time the ERA was being hotly debated in the country, the Court ignited another hot debate with its 1973 *Roe v. Wade* decision. It was one of the most controversial cases in the Court's history. In

Justice Harry Blackmun

pregnancy, a woman and her doctor had the right to decide whether the woman should have an abortion. During the second trimester, when abortion becomes somewhat risky, the state could regulate abortions to ensure women's safety. After the fetus becomes viable (in other words, able to live outside the womb), which occurs after roughly six months, the state could prohibit an abortion if it chose, except when the procedure was necessary to save a woman's life or to preserve her health.

The euphoria with which many in the women's rights movement greeted the *Roe v. Wade* decision soon turned to dismay. The ERA, which was so close to ratification, stalled. Senator Ervin worked closely with anti-ratificationists and used his privileges as a senator to mail, without paying postage, packets of information against the ERA to representatives in key states that were voting on the amendment. By 1982, only one additional state had ratified the ERA, while a number of states that had accepted it voted to rescind their ratification. The ERA was dead.

Now the only avenue to expand women's equal rights as a constitutional matter was the Supreme Court. Indeed,

a seven-to-two decision, the Court held that women had a constitutional right to choose to have an abortion.

In 1965, the Court had struck down, in *Griswold v. Connecticut*, a Connecticut law that prohibited the distribution of information about contraceptives. The Court had ruled then that various provisions of the Constitution guaranteed a right to privacy in certain personal matters.

Justice Harry A. Blackmun, who wrote the majority opinion in *Roe v. Wade*, used the 1965 opinion to establish a constitutional right to privacy with regard to abortion. He ruled that during approximately the first three months (first trimester) of

In the three decades since *Roe v. Wade*, the Supreme Court has issued numerous additional decisions refining the *Roe* decision. As the composition of the Supreme Court has changed, so has the Court's interpretation of a woman's constitutional right to privacy and her freedom to determine whether to carry a pregnancy. The Court has never overturned *Roe v. Wade* but has upheld numerous restrictions that various states have placed on obtaining an abortion.

some opponents of the ERA had argued that the ERA was not necessary because the Equal Protection Clause provided sufficient guarantees of equal treatment of men and women by federal and state governments. They also pointed out that the Supreme Court had started to strike down sex-discriminatory laws. The High Court did not, however, strike down all laws that treated men and women differently.

In 1981, it upheld in a six-to-three vote the constitutionality of a California law that made it a crime for any male to have sex with a female under the age of eighteen. The law did not, however, make it a crime for females to have sex with males under the age of eighteen. The defendant, Michael M., was seventeen and a half years old when he had sexual intercourse with a six-teen-and-a-half-year-old female. He was charged with "statutory rape."

The Court in 1981 also upheld the Selective Service Act, which required men, but not women, to register for the draft.

In 1982, the Court did strike down the women-only admissions policy of the Mississippi University for Women by a vote of five to four. MUW had a four-year baccalaureate program in nursing. Joe Hogan, a registered nurse who worked as a nursing supervisor in a medical center, applied for admission to the MUW School of Nursing's baccalaureate program in 1979. MUW was in Columbus, Mississippi, where Hogan lived and worked. By attending MUW, he could continue working as a nursing supervisor at a local hospital and wouldn't have to give up his job to go to one of Mississippi's other two coed nursing schools, which were out of town.

MUW turned Hogan down solely because he was male. School officials told him that he could audit courses but couldn't enroll for credit.

Newly appointed Justice Sandra Day O'Connor, who wrote the majority opinion, said that MUW's all-women policy violated the Fourteenth Amendment's Equal Protection Clause. She also ruled that there must be an "exceedingly persuasive justification" for any law that discriminated based on gender.

In 1996, building on Justice O'Connor's 1982 decision, the Court issued its historic

84

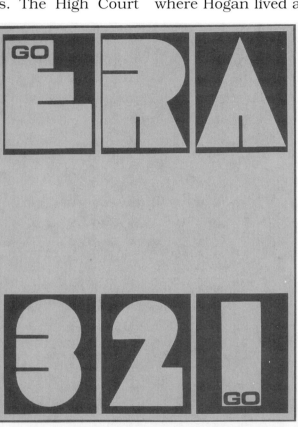

Poster supporting the Equal Rights Amendment (circa 1965)

Appointed in 1981 by President Ronald Reagan, Justice Sandra Day O'Connor was the first woman to serve as a justice of the U.S. Supreme Court. When she obtained her law degree in 1952 from Stanford University, she was unable to find employment in private law firms due to sex discrimination. She began her law career as a deputy county attorney in California, then worked for three years as an attorney for the U.S. Army in Germany. She later went into private practice, became an assistant attorney general in Arizona, and was appointed and then elected to the Arizona Senate, becoming majority leader from 1973 to 1974. She then was appointed as a trial judge, and in 1979 was appointed to the Arizona Appeals Court.

produce citizen-soldiers, "educated and honorable men, prepared for the varied work of civil life, imbued with love of learning, confident in the functions and attitudes of leadership, possessing a high sense of public service, advocates of American democracy and the free enterprise system," who would be prepared to defend the country in time of national peril. To accomplish this, it required its uniformed cadets to live in Spartan barracks, without any privacy, and to go through a form of training similar to boot camp in the marines. VMI also used the "adversative method" of teaching, in which students were forced to doubt their previous beliefs and experiences.

In 1990, the U.S. government sued the state of Virginia and VMI, arguing that its male-only policy violated the Equal Protection Clause. A female high school student, who wanted to attend VMI but was unable to do so because the school refused to admit women, had filed a complaint with the U.S. attorney general. After investigation, the Justice Department, an arm of the attorney general, decided to file suit against VMI. This student was not the only female who wanted to attend VMI. During the two years before the lawsuit was filed, 347 female students had written to VMI expressing an interest in attending; none of them had received any reply.

The federal district judge hearing the case ruled in VMI's favor, stating that VMI brought diversity to Virginia's colleges by adding an all-male institution to an otherwise coeducational college system. He also said that admitting women to VMI would

decision in the case of *United States v. Virginia.* The case involved the constitutionality of the exclusion of women from one of the state's colleges, the Virginia Military Institute (VMI). The mission of VMI was to

Virginia Women's Institute for Leadership student Kristin Van Wegin on a tour of the Virginia Military Institute campus (1995)

force the school to change its educational methods to accommodate women cadets. It would have to provide some personal privacy, adjust its physical-education requirements, and tone down its adversative method of instruction.

The federal Court of Appeals reversed the district judge's decision. It stated that Virginia had three options: (a) admit women to VMI, (b) establish a parallel institution or program for women, or (c) stop providing state support for VMI.

Virginia then established the Virginia Women's Institute for Leadership (VWIL). VWIL offered different courses, did not have degree programs in the sciences and engineering as did VMI, and had fewer resources than VMI. It also did not use the adversative method of education and did not use boot-camp-like physical training. Graduating from VWIL did not give a woman the same status and job opportunities as graduating from VMI, a college that was established in 1839.

The district court judge approved Virginia's two-college plan. The appeals court upheld that decision. The courts ruled that Virginia did not have to provide a mirror image of VMI for women at VWIL. As long as VWIL and VMI were "substantially comparable," Virginia did not violate the Equal Protection Clause by having different schools for men and women. The district court and appeals court essentially adopted a "separate but comparable" standard of equality for women.

Remember, in *Brown v. Board of Education* the Supreme Court had ruled that separate was *not* equal: "We conclude that in the field of public education the doctrine of 'separate but equal' has no place. Separate educational facilities are inherently unequal."

The Supreme Court agreed to hear the case. Because the Court had previously struck down the single-sex admissions policy of the Mississippi University for Women, it would seem clear that the Court would strike down Virginia's plan. But the college in Virginia that excluded women was a military institute. Moreover, Virginia had established a separate college for women. Using the Supreme Court's own standard for reviewing sex-discriminatory policies, the appeals court had concluded that Virginia had provided an "exceedingly persuasive" justification for VMI remaining

President Bill Clinton appointed Justice Ruth Bader Ginsburg as the second woman to the Supreme Court in 1993. She attended both Harvard and Columbia law schools, graduating in 1959. Thereafter, she clerked for a judge of the U.S. District Court in New York, and then taught at several law schools. In 1972, she founded the Women's Rights Project and served as its counsel until 1980, when she was appointed to the U.S. Court of Appeals for the District of Columbia Circuit by President Jimmy Carter.

male-only. The Supreme Court had displayed a willingness to accept sex discrimination by the military (for example, the draft-registration case previously mentioned), and the appeals court had approved Virginia's two-college plan, so the outcome of the case was not predictable.

Nevertheless, by a seven-to-one vote, the Supreme Court struck down Virginia's two-college program. Justice Ruth Bader Ginsburg wrote the majority opinion.

The High Court ruled that the state of Virginia violated the Equal Protection Clause by totally excluding women from VMI while not providing women with equal opportunity at VWIL. It held that there was no "exceedingly persuasive justification" for the exclusion of women from VMI.

How did the Supreme Court, using the same standard of review and considering the same facts, arrive at a different conclusion than had the appeals court? Among other factors, it may be that having two women on the Court heavily influenced the Supreme Court's view of the case. Both female justices were well acquainted with the history of sex discrimination. Justice

Ginsburg, a feminist jurist, had written extensively on sex discrimination and the Equal Protection Clause even before she became a justice of the Supreme Court.

Justice Ginsburg pointed out that when the state of Virginia established VMI in 1839, it did not do so in order to provide "diversity" in its educational system. There was no diversity in Virginia's higher education at the time, because only men could attend college in Virginia.

The Supreme Court then addressed Virginia's argument that the adversative method of education would be destroyed if VMI was made coeducational. The district court had acknowledged that some women could meet all the standards that VMI imposes on male cadets, and that some women would prefer VMI's adversative method to other forms of education. Nevertheless, the court had used generalizations about men and women (supposedly men thrive in an adversative atmosphere, whereas women thrive in a cooperative one) to approve VMI as an all-male college. The High Court stated that it was inappropriate to use broad generalizations about men and women to perpetuate a historical

88

Justice Ginsburg wrote:
The notion that admission of women would downgrade VMI's stature, destroy the adversative system and, with it, even the school, is . . . a prediction hardly different from other "self-fulfilling prophec[ies]" once routinely used to deny rights or opportunities. . . . Medical faculties similarly resisted men and women partners in the study of medicine. . . . More recently, women seeking careers in policing encountered resistance based on fears that their presence would "undermine male solidarity," deprive male partners of adequate assistance and lead to sexual misconduct. Field studies did not confirm these fears. Women's successful entry into the federal military academies, and their participation in the Nation's military forces, indicate that Virginia's fears for the future of VMI may not be solidly grounded.

pattern of discrimination and to deny admission to women who could meet the VMI standards. The Court also disagreed with predictions that the admission of women to VMI would destroy its adversative method.

Justice Ginsburg then addressed Virginia's two-college solution. She found the separate colleges under the plan (VMI and VWIL) to be unequal. She called VWIL "a 'pale shadow' of VMI."

The Supreme Court therefore struck down, as a violation of the Equal Protection Clause, the exclusion of women from VMI and Virginia's plan of providing an alternate education for women at VWIL.

The Supreme Court's decision leaves open the question of whether a state could legitimately establish two new colleges (or two new high schools)—one exclusively for males and one exclusively for females—as long as they were substantively equal. Since the Court has struck down "separate but equal" in the context of race, will it allow "separate but equal" in the context of gender? What about the disabled? Should persons with disabilities have equal protection under the law?

"A Regime of State-Mandated Segregation and Degradation": Does the Equal Protection Clause Apply to People with Disabilities?

The Constitution Says . . .
"No State shall . . . deny to any person within its jurisdiction the equal protection of the laws."
—U.S. Constitution, Amendment XIV, Section 1

10

Carrie Buck and her mother, Emma Buck

Persons with both physical and mental disabilities have experienced enormous discrimination and encountered barriers that impede, and in some cases block, their full and equal participation in American society.

In colonial days and into the nineteenth century, many people with disabilities were warehoused in miserable almshouses. These were institutions where poor people, mentally and physically disabled people, and criminals were often housed together. Even so, by the early part of the nineteenth century, there was recognition that at least some disabled people could be integrated into society. Education opportunities became available for some.

A school for the blind was opened in Baltimore in 1812. Five years later, Thomas Hopkins Gallaudet began a school for the deaf in Hartford, Connecticut, called the American Asylum for the Deaf and Dumb. Still, most disabled people were simply left in institutions without any education or training.

Unlike other minorities, the disabled population was not politically organized. Even when the Civil War resulted in the disability of thousands of veterans, they were unable to effectively bring about changes in the way they were treated. The first glimmers of a disability rights movement appeared toward the end of the nineteenth century, as blind and deaf people organized advocacy groups. They were successful in obtaining passage of relief laws for the blind.

World War I resulted in another surge in the numbers of physically disabled people. In addition, with the industrialization of America, there were increasing numbers who became disabled from workplace injuries. By 1920, Congress had passed laws providing funding for vocational training for the handicapped.

The first Supreme Court case involving a disabled person was the 1927 *Buck v. Bell* decision. The case involved the compulsory sterilization of people alleged to be mentally retarded. It epitomized the stubbornly persistent negative stereotypes about people who were considered disabled.

The backdrop to the Court's decision was a concept called "scientific racism," which developed in the late nineteenth century. Although there is no scientific basis for racism, those supporting this concept claimed that intelligence and character were hereditary and not influenced by education or the environment. IQ (intelligence quotient) tests were developed in the early twentieth century to determine children's reasoning ability so that those children who scored low on the tests could be given special education to improve their abilities. However, the IQ tests became used in the United States to rank children by intelligence levels.

Eugenics became a popular movement in the United States and other parts of the world. The eugenicists' goal was to breed a perfect race of people, based on the concepts of "scientific racism." Although eugenics had developed as a science to improve cattle, racehorses, and show animals by selective breeding, eugenicists applied these concepts to human beings.

They believed that intelligence, social

91

The nation's most famous disabled person was President Franklin D. Roosevelt (center), who was unable to walk as a result of polio. However, Roosevelt hid this fact from the public, something he probably could not have done if there had been television when he was president in the 1930s and 1940s. He was never seen in public in his wheelchair. Here he is flanked by Winston Churchill (left) and Joseph Stalin (right) in this 1945 photograph of the Crimean Conference.

pulsory eugenic sterilization laws between 1907 and 1931.

One of the many states that enacted such a sterilization law was Virginia. Carrie Buck, a seventeen-year-old woman, was committed to the State Colony for Epileptics and Feeble Minded in Lynchburg, Virginia, shortly after she had given birth to a daughter, on the grounds that she was feebleminded. Her mother had also been committed to the institution as feebleminded. Carrie and her mother, Emma Buck, were given IQ tests, which allegedly showed that Carrie had a mental age of nine years and her mother a mental age below eight years. Based on these results, the colony's board of directors ordered Carrie Buck to be sterilized, but Buck's guardian filed suit contesting the order.

To support its argument for the sterilization of Carrie Buck, the state of Virginia presented the testimony of Harry Laughlin, an employee of the Virginia Eugenics Records Office. He reviewed the information he had about Carrie Buck, her mother, and her infant daughter. *Without ever seeing them or interviewing them*, he concluded that Carrie Buck's "feeblemindedness" was primarily hereditary, and that she was a member of the "shiftless, ignorant, and worthless class of antisocial whites of the South." Another employee of the record office gave Carrie's infant daughter, Vivian, a mental test and concluded that she was below average.

The state of Virginia also presented testimony from a Red Cross worker who had placed Vivian Buck in a foster home. She

behavior, and many mental and physical illnesses were purely genetic—passed from parents to child. Their work was based on the premise that whites were superior to other races, and that the goal of society and science should be to create a pure and perfect race of people—in their view, a white race. They also supported the use of IQ tests to identify "mentally inferior" individuals.

Use of IQ tests became common throughout the United States after World War I. Eugenicists argued that feebleminded people should not have children and should be sterilized. They also wanted to prohibit interracial marriage because they presumed that the offspring would be "inferior." Twenty-nine states enacted com-

testified that the daughter (a mere seven months old at the time of the visit) had a "look" about her that was "not quite normal." Based on evidence such as this, the judge authorized the sterilization of Carrie Buck.

On appeal, Buck's attorney argued that the sterilization statute violated the Due Process and Equal Protection clauses of the Fourteenth Amendment. He argued that it violated Due Process to mutilate a person's reproductive organs, and that under the Equal Protection Clause, the state could not treat mentally retarded people differently from other people.

The Supreme Court, in a four-page, eight-to-one opinion written by Justice Oliver Wendell Holmes, upheld the sterilization order. He wrote:

The Virginia Colony for Epileptics and Feeble Minded, Lynchburg, Virginia

It is better for all the world, if instead of waiting to execute degenerate offspring for crime, or to let them starve for their imbecility, society can prevent those who are manifestly unfit from continuing their kind. . . . Three generations of imbeciles are enough.

With the law upheld, the state of Virginia proceeded to sterilize over 7,500 people during the next several decades, including Carrie's sister, Doris. In addition to the "feebleminded," it sterilized those who exhibited "antisocial behavior," including unwed mothers, children with disciplinary problems, prostitutes, and petty criminals.

But Carrie Buck was *not* retarded. When Carrie and Doris were interviewed more than fifty years later, neither showed any indication of being mentally retarded. They lacked formal education but not intelligence. Doris Buck had wanted very much to have children, and she and her husband had tried for many years for her to become pregnant. Not until reporters told her during the interview that she had been sterilized did she know why she had never been able to have children.

While in mid-twentieth-century America those deemed retarded faced draconian measures and exclusion from society, there were efforts to integrate those with physical disabilities into the mainstream. During World War II, Dr. Howard Rusk and Dr. Henry Kessler established the field of rehabilitation medicine and set up rehabilitation centers. In 1947, President Harry S. Truman established the President's

Justice Oliver Wendell Holmes

Committee on Employment of the Handicapped, with the goal of encouraging businesses to hire disabled people after they had completed rehabilitation. Both of these efforts focused on those with *physical* disabilities.

Nevertheless, there was still enormous prejudice against those with physical disabilities. Until the 1960s, some municipalities had "ugly laws," which prohibited those who were deformed or maimed from being in public. Many cities had separate schools for students with disabilities, or where there were no such schools, they had to be taught at home.

Moreover, people with disabilities faced numerous physical barriers. How could a

94

person in a wheelchair get into a building that had steps but no ramps? How could a child in a wheelchair go to school? How could a person in a wheelchair eat in restaurants, or use buses or subways? And even if a person could get into a building, if the bathroom entrance door or stall door were too small for wheelchairs, he or she would have no way to use the restroom facilities.

The deaf or hearing impaired found it difficult to participate fully in conferences or concerts without a sign language interpreter. There were no captions for deaf viewers on any television programs until 1971, and it still took years for a significant number of programs to be captioned. Many programs still do not have captions.

Blind people faced resistance to bringing guide dogs into stores and onto airplanes.

Two generations after the *Buck v. Bell* decision, an organized disability rights movement began to emerge. Ed Roberts, a quadriplegic man who had been disabled by polio, was one of the spark plugs who ignited the emerging disability rights movement. In the early 1960s, he applied to the University of California at Berkeley. California's Department of Rehabilitation, which paid for college education for disabled students, refused to pay for his college education. The reason? It claimed that it would be a waste of money because Roberts would never be able to work. Roberts went to the press, and after receiving a lot of negative publicity, the rehabilitation department relented and agreed to pay for his education.

Although the word "handicapped" is used in many laws pertaining to disabled people, these individuals generally prefer the phrase "persons with disabilities." The focus, then, is on the person and not on the particular disability.

Roberts's next obstacle was getting admitted to Berkeley. A dean there told him, "We've tried cripples before and it didn't work." Besides the dean's attitude, another obstacle was Roberts' eight-hundred-pound iron lung, where he slept and spent part of each day. It was too heavy for the floors in the dormitory. He successfully overcame these hurdles. The director of student services said Roberts could live on the third floor of the hospital, which had floors strong enough for his iron lung. Roberts had friends and paid attendants to help him with dressing and eating, and they also pushed his wheelchair.

Soon other students who were severely disabled from polio or spinal cord injuries joined Roberts on the third floor of the university's hospital. They began calling themselves the Rolling Quads.

Although the Rolling Quads had wheelchairs, they were unable to leave the campus because their wheelchairs could not go over the five-inch curbs common in Berkeley. They demanded that the city put ramps on the city streets, a demand that they won after showing up at a city council meeting in their wheelchairs.

The students followed this victory with plans to live independently. They wanted to be part of mainstream society, rather than be segregated in separate quarters. Yet it was extremely difficult to find apartments that were wheelchair accessible. Moreover, at that time, wheelchairs weren't very sturdy, so the students began developing stronger ones.

Roberts not only graduated from college, but by 1971, he was dean of students and professor of political science at Common College. Moreover, in 1975, California governor Jerry Brown appointed him director of the California Department of Rehabilitation because of his leadership in the emerging disability rights movement. This was the same department that had concluded many years before that Roberts would never be able to work!

On the national level, a federal law passed whose primary purpose was to provide grants to train those with disabilities to make them employable. Tucked away in the Rehabilitation Act of 1973 was a "Miscellaneous" title of the law. Within this obscure title, which attracted little notice in Congress, was the first major federal disability rights law. Discrimination against disabled people by any program or activity that received federal financial assistance was prohibited. This meant not only that federal agencies could not discriminate against qualified people who had disabilities but also that federal contractors, public universities, and any other institutions receiving federal funds also could not discriminate. Moreover, the new law required federal contractors to use affirmative action to hire and promote persons with disabilities.

Two years later, in 1975, Congress passed the Education for All Handicapped Children Act. At that time, over half of the 8 million disabled children in the United States did not receive proper educational services, and 1 million of them were totally excluded from public schools. This act assured that disabled children would have a free, appropriate public education.

With more awareness of disability discrimination, the Supreme Court shifted its attitudes as well. In 1985, almost sixty years after the *Buck* decision, the Supreme Court issued its next decision involving the rights of mentally retarded people.

The city of Cleburne, Texas, had refused to grant the Cleburne Living Center a permit to open a group home for the mentally retarded. Property owners opposed the proposal and expressed concerns about housing retarded people so near their homes. The Supreme Court ruled in its 1985 *Cleburne* decision that the city's refusal to allow the group home in this particular case rested on "irrational prejudice" against mentally retarded people and therefore violated the Equal Protection Clause.

Despite the recent advances, two-thirds of disabled people were still unemployed in 1988. In that year, the Americans with Disabilities Act (ADA) was introduced in Congress. It was the most comprehensive disability rights bill ever. Because there were 43 million people with impairments of some kind in the United States, many members of Congress had a close family member or friend who had a disability, or they themselves had a disability. Even the president, George H. W. Bush, had lost a three-year-old daughter to leukemia and had a son with a severe learning disability, another son who had had part of his colon removed, and an uncle who was a quadriplegic from polio. Disability rights groups, which had often acted independently of one another, worked together to get the ADA passed.

Nevertheless, because of opposition from parts of the business community that did not want to hire people with disabilities or feared the costs of accommodating the needs of workers with disabilities, the bill took two years to pass Congress. But as several large corporations told of their positive experiences with hiring persons with disabilities, opposition to the bill lost steam. By 1990, both the House and the Senate voted overwhelmingly for the bill, and President Bush signed it into law on July 26, 1990.

The ADA law prohibits employment discrimination based on physical or mental disability. It requires employers to provide reasonable accommodations for disabled workers who are otherwise qualified, as long as this will not cause "undue hardship" to the employers.

One Hundred First Congress of the United States of America

AT THE SECOND SESSION

Begun and held at the City of Washington on Tuesday, the twenty-third day of January, one thousand nine hundred and ninety

An Act

To establish a clear and comprehensive prohibition of discrimination on the basis of disability.

Be it enacted by the Senate and House of Representatives of the United States of America in Congress assembled,

SECTION 1. SHORT TITLE; TABLE OF CONTENTS.

(a) SHORT TITLE.—This Act may be cited as the "Americans with Disabilities Act of 1990".

(b) TABLE OF CONTENTS.—The table of contents is as follows:

Sec. 1. Short title; table of contents.
Sec. 2. Findings and purposes.
Sec. 3. Definitions.

TITLE I—EMPLOYMENT

Sec. 101. Definitions.
Sec. 102. Discrimination.
Sec. 103. Defenses.
Sec. 104. Illegal use of drugs and alcohol.
Sec. 105. Posting notices.
Sec. 106. Regulations.
Sec. 107. Enforcement.
Sec. 108. Effective date.

TITLE II—PUBLIC SERVICES

Subtitle A—Prohibition Against Discrimination and Other Generally Applicable Provisions

Sec. 201. Definition.
Sec. 202. Discrimination.
Sec. 203. Enforcement.
Sec. 204. Regulations.
Sec. 205. Effective date.

Subtitle B—Actions Applicable to Public Transportation Provided by Public Entities Considered Discriminatory

PART I—PUBLIC TRANSPORTATION OTHER THAN BY AIRCRAFT OR CERTAIN RAIL OPERATIONS

Sec. 221. Definitions.
Sec. 222. Public entities operating fixed route systems.
Sec. 223. Paratransit as a complement to fixed route service.
Sec. 224. Public entity operating a demand responsive system.
Sec. 225. Temporary relief where lifts are unavailable.
Sec. 226. New facilities.
Sec. 227. Alterations of existing facilities.
Sec. 228. Public transportation programs and activities in existing facilities and one car per train rule.
Sec. 229. Regulations.
Sec. 230. Interim accessibility requirements.
Sec. 231. Effective date.

PART II—PUBLIC TRANSPORTATION BY INTERCITY AND COMMUTER RAIL

Sec. 241. Definitions.
Sec. 242. Intercity and commuter rail actions considered discriminatory.
Sec. 243. Conformance of accessibility standards.

The Americans with Disabilities Act of 1990

The ADA also prohibits disability discrimination in public accommodations, such as hotels, restaurants, theaters, and recreational facilities. It generally does not, however, require building owners to make major structural changes so that buildings become accessible to those using wheelchairs or walkers. Only if an owner is renovating the building extensively does he or she have to include structural changes for accessibility. The law also requires all telephone companies to provide telephone services to hearing- and speech-impaired people so that they may communicate by telephone with others. Congress also made the ADA applicable to state and local governments.

The Supreme Court, however, has interpreted the ADA narrowly in employment cases. In 1999, a case reached the Court involving twin sisters who were extremely nearsighted without glasses (20/200 in the better eye, 20/400 in the worse eye) but who had 20/20 vision with glasses. United Airlines had refused to hire them as airline pilots because it required its pilots to have at least 20/100 vision without glasses.

The ADA defines the term "disability" as follows:

(a) having a "physical or mental impairment that substantially limits one or more major life activities," or

(b) having a history of such an impairment, or

(c) being considered to have such an impairment (even if the person is not in fact impaired).

In a seven-to-two decision in *Sutton v. United Air Lines,* the Supreme Court upheld United's refusal to hire the women. Justice Sandra Day O'Connor, who wrote the majority opinion, interpreted the definition of "disability" in the ADA to mean that a person is not disabled if he or she has corrected or lessened the disability (for example, by wearing eyeglasses to correct nearsightedness or taking medicine to reduce high blood pressure).

Justice John Paul Stevens (joined by Justice Stephen Breyer) dissented. He argued that the Court's interpretation led to a "bizarre result": that when a person overcomes his or her disability and therefore becomes more employable, that person loses the protections against disability discrimination that Congress intended to provide when it passed the ADA. He also argued that the Court's decision meant that United could refuse to hire the sisters, even if its refusal was "purely on the basis of irrational fear and stereotype."

In 2001, the Court further limited the reach of the ADA. The case involved two

Chief Justice William Rehnquist

employees of the state of Alabama. Patricia Garrett was director of nursing, OB/GYN/Neonatal Services, for the University of Alabama at Birmingham Hospital. In 1994, she was diagnosed with breast cancer. Her surgery, radiation, and chemotherapy forced her to take substantial time off from work. When she returned to work in July 1995, she was removed from her position as director of nursing and transferred to a lower-paying job as a nurse manager.

Milton Ash worked as a security officer for the Alabama Department of Youth Services. He told the department that he had chronic asthma, and at his doctor's recommendation asked the department to modify his job duties to minimize his exposure to carbon monoxide and cigarette smoke. Ash later was diagnosed with sleep apnea (a medical disorder that causes repeated disruptions of sleep). On his doctor's advice, he asked the department to reassign him to the day shift. Although the ADA requires an employer to make reasonable accommodations for workers with disabilities if the accommodations won't be an undue hardship for the employer, the department refused to comply with either of Ash's requests.

Both Garrett and Ash filed suit against the state of Alabama, claiming it had violated the ADA. Alabama argued that Congress did not have the constitutional authority to allow states to be sued under the ADA. In a five-to-four decision written by Chief Justice William H. Rehnquist, the Court agreed with Alabama in *Board of Trustees, University of Alabama v. Garrett.* Chief Justice Rehnquist said that there was not enough evidence of a history of disability discrimination by states for Congress to authorize lawsuits against state governments. He wrote:

> States are not required by the Fourteenth Amendment to make special accommodations for the disabled, so long as their actions toward such individuals are rational. They could quite hardheadedly—perhaps hardheartedly—hold to job-qualification requirements which do not make allowance for the disabled.

He also said it would be "entirely rational (and therefore constitutional) for a state employer to conserve scarce financial resources by hiring employees who are able to use existing facilities" instead of making the facilities accessible to the disabled.

Justice Breyer, joined by three other justices, wrote a dissenting opinion in which he argued that Congress had significant evidence of disability discrimination by state governments. He also argued that the Court was imposing an unreasonably high standard of evidence on Congress before it could pass laws to enforce Section 1 of the Fourteenth Amendment.

In 2002, the Supreme Court once again narrowed the ADA. Ella Williams worked for Toyota on an assembly line in Kentucky. She developed carpal tunnel syndrome and tendinitis as a result of her assembly-line job. Her doctor ordered that she not lift more than twenty pounds, do repetitive work involving bending her wrists or elbows, do overhead work, or use tools that vibrate. Toyota modified her work duties, but she continued to have difficulty performing her job. She eventually filed suit, claiming that Toyota had not made "reasonable accommodation" for her disability, as required by the ADA. She argued that she was disabled because she had a physical impairment that substantially limited her ability to do a major life activity—namely, manual tasks.

In a unanimous opinion written by Justice Sandra Day O'Connor, the Court held in *Toyota Motor Mfg., Ky., Inc. v. Williams* that for a person to be considered disabled with regard to manual tasks under the ADA, the evidence must show that the person cannot do the manual tasks that most people do on a day-to-day basis (for example, household chores and bathing). The fact that Williams was unable to perform the tasks involved at her particular job at Toyota was *not* sufficient to prove that she had a disability under the ADA. That is, Williams's impairments did not qualify as a "disability" under the ADA because they did not "substantially limit" any "major life activity." Therefore, she was not entitled to bring suit against Toyota under the ADA.

In the past thirty years, Congress and the Supreme Court have ameliorated the more extreme barriers and prejudices faced by disabled people. Many buildings are now more accessible. There are more curb cuts at the corners of many city streets, allowing people in wheelchairs to move from the sidewalk to the street without going over a curb. (Curb cuts are not helpful to all disabled people, though. Blind people, for example, generally do not like curb cuts because a curb helps them figure out where a sidewalk ends.) Under the ADA, lawsuits can be brought against building owners or managers who violate the accessibility requirements, or against employers who discriminate against those considered, according to the Supreme Court's decisions, to be disabled.

But the barriers and discrimination faced by people with disabilities are still substantial. A major limitation of the ADA is that it does not give any federal agency the authority to implement the provisions of the act. If the law is violated, the only way to enforce it is through lawsuits, a time-consuming, expensive method of enforcement. Seventy percent of severely disabled people are still unemployed. Many office buildings, even government buildings, remain inaccessible to those in wheelchairs. Only time will tell whether people with physical or mental disabilities will be given the opportunity to participate in society to the full extent of their abilities.

"THE CONSTITUTION NEITHER KNOWS NOR TOLERATES CLASSES AMONG CITIZENS": SHOULD SEXUAL MINORITIES BE ENTITLED TO EQUAL RIGHTS?

THE CONSTITUTION SAYS . . .
"NO STATE SHALL . . . DENY TO ANY PERSON WITHIN ITS JURISDICTION THE EQUAL PROTECTION OF THE LAWS."
—U.S. CONSTITUTION, AMENDMENT XIV, SECTION 1

"CONGRESS SHALL MAKE NO LAW . . . ABRIDGING THE FREEDOM OF SPEECH . . . OR THE RIGHT OF THE PEOPLE PEACEABLY TO ASSEMBLE. . . ."
—U.S. CONSTITUTION, AMENDMENT I

11

Christopher Street Liberation Day, New York City (1973)

Gay men and lesbians have existed throughout history. Such people include nineteenth-century poet Walt Whitman; twentieth-century writers James Baldwin, Gertrude Stein, and Audre Lorde; civil rights activist Bayard Rustin (who helped organize the 1963 March on Washington), tennis star Martina Navratilova, and singer Melissa Etheridge.

However, at the beginning of the twentieth century, most gay people were "closeted," that is, hiding the fact that their primary attraction was to people of the same sex and pretending in public that they were heterosexual.

Gay people first began to organize in the United States in 1924, when Henry Gerber, a Bavarian immigrant, formed the first gay rights organization in this country. The group folded after only a year, however, when publicity about it resulted in harassment of its members and the loss of Mr. Gerber's post office job for "conduct unbecoming a postal worker."

World War II fostered the development of the modern gay and lesbian movements. Although the armed forces had an official policy of excluding and discharging gay people, many gay men and lesbians in fact served in the military during the war. The war brought isolated homosexual people in contact with each other through military service.

The end of World War II precipitated "witch hunts" to root out and discharge gay soldiers because the government no longer needed as many people in the military. "Undesirable discharges," which were issued to many homosexual service members, prevented gay veterans from receiving health, pension, and unemployment benefits, and made it difficult for them to find jobs. In 1945, the Veterans Benevolent Association was founded. For almost a decade, the organization provided support and a social network for gay and lesbian veterans.

After the war, gay men and lesbians began migrating to major cities such as San Francisco and New York, where they could live in larger supportive communities. Bars and clubs that catered to the gay community began to appear.

The rise of the Cold War and the McCarthy era in the 1950s resulted in more antigay witch hunts. Gay men and lesbians discovered to be working in government agencies were fired because politicians accused homosexuals of being "subversives."

While gay men and lesbians have served in the military for years, many with distinction, they still must keep their sexual orientation a secret. The current policy of the U.S. military, adopted in 1993, is "Don't ask, don't tell." This means that the military no longer asks recruits or soldiers if they are gay or lesbian. However, if a soldier discloses ("tells") that he or she is gay, or if the military otherwise learns that a soldier is gay, then the soldier can be discharged. The Center for the Study of Sexual Minorities in the Military estimates that about 60,000 members of the armed forces are "closeted" gays or lesbians, that is, soldiers who are keeping their gay identity a secret. Over one thousand soldiers are discharged each year after their homosexuality is discovered. Only two NATO members—Turkey and the United States—still ban known homosexuals from serving in the armed forces.

In the face of increasing attacks, gay and lesbian organizations began forming in the early 1950s. These groups provided members with a supportive environment in which to meet and help each other cope in an often hostile world. Because of the pervasive antigay attitudes of the times, these organizations were secretive, and many members used pseudonyms to hide their identities. The two major groups at the time were the Mattachine Society, founded in 1950 in Los Angeles by Harry Hay and other gay men, and Daughters of Bilitis, formed in 1955 in San Francisco by Del Martin, Phyllis Lyon, and six other lesbians. By the early 1960s, both of these organizations had chapters in several other large cities.

Not until 1965, however, did the first large-scale gay rights demonstration occur, when lesbian and gay activists picketed the Pentagon, the White House, and numerous federal agencies to protest employment discrimination against gay men and lesbians.

The modern gay and lesbian movement was born in 1969 out of the Stonewall riots. Gay and lesbian bars had faced routine police raids and arrests of their patrons. The raid of the Stonewall Inn in New York City's Greenwich Village in the early morning hours of June 28, 1969, was no different than many other police raids around the country. What set this one apart was the reaction of the patrons. Both the customers and the female impersonators performing at the Stonewall Inn fought back, refusing to accept another raid and more arrests. The riots lasted several days, involving more than a thousand people. The Mattachine Society circulated leaflets condemning police harassment. The gay and lesbian community held organizing meetings and protest marches.

After the Stonewall riots, gay and lesbian activists (many of whom had been involved in the civil rights or antiwar movements) formed new literary, cultural, and social service organizations for their communities. Gay and lesbian newspapers helped spread the news of the growing movement to those isolated from the centers of gay and lesbian activism. Increasing numbers of gay men and lesbians came out of the closet, openly acknowledging their homosexuality. Every June, a growing number organized and participated in gay pride festivals and marches in communities around the country to

Pride Day, New York City (1971)

commemorate the Stonewall riots.

By 1979, gay and lesbian activists had grown sufficiently in number to hold the first National March for Gay and Lesbian Rights in Washington, D.C. The march drew between 100,000 and 200,000 people. During the march weekend, the first National Third World Lesbian and Gay Conference was held, which led to the founding of the National Coalition of Black Gays.

But what propelled the struggle for gay and lesbian civil rights into a large nationwide movement was, ironically, an antigay 1986 Supreme Court decision, *Bowers v. Hardwick*. Michael Hardwick, a gay man who was arrested while having sexual relations with another man in the bedroom of his home and was charged with sodomy, filed suit against the state of Georgia. Georgia's sodomy law prohibited certain types of sexual expression by both homosexual and heterosexual couples, even in the privacy of a home. Hardwick challenged the law based on the constitutional right to privacy.

There had been previous antigay decisions by the Court. In 1967, for example, the Court ruled six to three that the United States could deport a gay Canadian, Clive Michael Boutilier, solely because of his homosexuality. Boutilier had become a permanent resident in the United States when he was twenty-one years old, living and working in New York City for a decade. Boutilier's mother, his stepfather, and three of his siblings were residents in the United States. When Boutilier applied for U.S. citizenship, however, the Immigration and Naturalization Service (INS) said he should be deported to Canada because of his homosexuality. It relied on a federal law that excluded those aliens "afflicted with [a] psychopathic personality," arguing that this phrase included homosexuals. Justice Tom C. Clark, writing for the majority of the Court, agreed: "We . . . conclude that the Congress used the phrase 'psychopathic personality' . . . to exclude from entry all homosexuals and other sex perverts."

And in 1976, the Court simply upheld, without writing any opinion, a Virginia criminal law that made sodomy a felony, even when sodomy occurred between consenting adults in the privacy of a home. Gay plaintiffs had challenged the law as a violation of privacy, freedom of expression, and due process.

Despite these adverse Court decisions, many gay men and lesbians expected a positive decision from the Court in 1986. There had been changes in social and professional attitudes about homosexuality. (In 1973, the American Psychiatric Association removed homosexuality from the list of mental illnesses, and in 1975 the American Psychological Association supported the decision of the American Psychiatric Association.) Moreover, the Court had been expanding the constitu-

Federal civil rights laws *do not* prohibit discrimination against gay men and lesbians in employment, housing, and public accommodations.

tional right to privacy since the 1960s.

Nevertheless, in a five-to-four decision, the Court upheld Georgia's sodomy law. The majority of the Supreme Court held that the constitutional right to privacy did not extend to homosexual relations. Justice Byron R. White, who wrote the majority opinion, argued that even to claim that liberty included the right to have sexual relations with a person of the same sex was "facetious." Chief Justice Warren Burger and Justices Lewis F. Powell Jr., William Rehnquist, and Sandra Day O'Connor joined Justice White's opinion.

Justice Harry Blackmun wrote an impassioned dissent, joined by Justices William J. Brennan Jr., Thurgood Marshall, and John Paul Stevens. He wrote that the case was not about "a fundamental right to engage in homosexual sodomy," as Justice White claimed. Instead, quoting from a dissenting opinion of Justice Louis D. Brandeis, Justice Blackmun wrote, "Rather, this case is about 'the most comprehensive of rights and the right most valued by civilized men,' namely, 'the right to be let alone.'"

The *Bowers* decision, which essentially upheld state laws that labeled gay men and lesbians as criminals, infuriated the gay community. The following year, gay and lesbian activists organized another march on Washington. This time, 500,000 people marched.

105

Copyright © Marc Geller

Former Boy Scout James Dale, San Francisco (1992)

The burgeoning gay rights movement included not just homosexuals but also heterosexual supporters. The most important heterosexual organization supporting the struggle for gay rights was Parents and Friends of Lesbians and Gays (PFLAG). PFLAG, founded in 1981, with Adele Starr as its first president, is a national organization that has support groups throughout the country for parents and family members who have a gay or lesbian relative. It has become a powerful education and advocacy group that supports equal rights for gay men and lesbians, with 460 chapters and 80,000 members. (Today it is called Parents, Families, and Friends of Lesbians and Gays.)

As opposition to homosexuality decreased, some cities and states passed laws prohibiting discrimination based on sexual orientation. The growing gay rights movement gave rise to a strong backlash movement, which sought to repeal any existing civil rights protection for sexual orientation and to prevent any further expansion of equal rights for gay people.

In 1992, the backlash movement succeeded in getting Colorado voters to approve an amendment to that state's constitution prohibiting any government in Colorado from adopting civil rights protections for gay men, lesbians, or bisexuals and from enforcing any such laws that already existed. This amendment was challenged in court.

The Colorado case, *Romer v. Evans*, was decided by the U.S. Supreme Court in 1996. The Court was considered significantly more conservative than it had been when it issued the *Bowers* decision. Of the three justices still on the Court who had voted on the *Bowers* case, two had voted to uphold the Georgia sodomy law. Three justices who had dissented in the *Bowers* case had left the Court (Justices Brennan, Marshall, and Blackmun). One of the justices appointed to the Court after *Bowers*, Anthony M. Kennedy, had written an appellate court decision in 1980 upholding the discharge of homosexuals from the navy. Two other new justices—Clarence Thomas and Antonin Scalia—generally sided with Chief Justice Rehnquist in decisions, and Rehnquist had voted in *Bowers* to uphold the Georgia sodomy law. Of the six justices appointed to the Court in the decade after the *Bowers* decision, only one, Ruth Bader Ginsburg, was considered more liberal than her predecessor.

Nevertheless, the explosive growth of the gay rights movement after the *Bowers* decision seemed to have an effect on the justices' attitudes toward gay rights. The Court ruled six to three that the Colorado constitutional amendment violated the Equal Protection Clause of the Fourteenth Amendment.

Quoting Justice John Harlan's dissent in the 1896 *Plessy* decision, Justice Kennedy wrote in the *Romer* decision, "[T]he Constitution 'neither knows nor tolerates classes among citizens.'" He ruled that the Colorado amendment did not serve any legitimate government purpose and that it violated the Equal Protection Clause by making gay people an unequal class. Justices John Paul Stevens, Sandra Day O'Connor, David H. Souter, Ruth Bader Ginsburg, and Stephen Breyer joined Justice Kennedy's opinion.

Justice Scalia, joined by Chief Justice Rehnquist and Justice Thomas, wrote a scathing dissent. Justice Scalia argued that, based on the 1986 *Bowers* decision, the Colorado amendment was constitutional. He accused the majority of taking sides in the "culture war."

In 2000, the Supreme Court rendered

another decision involving civil rights protections and sexual orientation in the *Boy Scouts of America v. Dale* case. This time, however, the Court ruled that the Boy Scouts of America could discriminate against gays and exclude them from the program. (The Girl Scouts of America does not exclude lesbians.)

James Dale joined the Cub Scouts in 1978 when he was eight years old. He became a Boy Scout three years later and remained in the organization until he was eighteen, reaching the rank of Eagle Scout. He then became an adult member of the Boy Scouts and an assistant scoutmaster. While in college, Dale served as copresident of the Rutgers University Lesbian/Gay Alliance. But he was expelled from the Boy Scouts when the head of the local troop learned from a newspaper article that Dale was gay.

Dale filed suit against the Boy Scouts in New Jersey state courts in 1992, maintaining that revoking his membership for being a gay man violated New Jersey's civil rights law. Part of that law prohibits discrimination in places of public accommodation on the basis of sexual orientation, among other categories. The New Jersey Supreme Court interpreted the law to apply to membership groups and ruled against the Boy Scouts. The Boy Scouts appealed.

The Supreme Court for many years had interpreted the First Amendment right of freedom to assemble as including the right to form clubs and organizations ("freedom of association"). However, the Court had ruled that state and local public accommodation laws prohibited large membership groups from discriminating on the basis of race or sex. Only when an organization was a purely private club (an "intimate association") or was formed for an "expressive purpose" (to advocate for a particular point of view) did civil rights laws not apply.

In 1984, the Supreme Court ruled seven to zero in *Roberts v. United States Jaycees* that Minnesota's human rights law meant that the Jaycees, a young men's organization with over 225,000 members, had to admit women as regular members. The Court concluded that Minnesota had a compelling interest in eradicating discrimination against women and that this justified some restrictions on freedom of association by the male members.

In 1987, the Supreme Court held in *Rotary International v. Rotary Club* that the Rotary Club, like the Jaycees, was not private enough to be exempt from civil rights laws and that the admission of women would not affect the activities of the group. Five years after the *Rotary* decision, James Dale filed his lawsuit against the Boy Scouts of America.

The New Jersey Supreme Court, relying on the *Rotary* decision, held that the Boy Scouts violated New Jersey's public accommodations laws by expelling Dale. It concluded that the Boy Scouts' large size (millions of members, including over a million adults), its nonselective manner of accepting new members, and its practice of allowing nonmembers to attend meetings showed that the organization was not sufficiently private to be protected under the First Amendment's freedom of association clause.

Justice John Paul Stevens

In 2000, the U.S. Supreme Court reversed the New Jersey Supreme Court in a five-to-four decision written by Chief Justice William Rehnquist. The Court held that applying New Jersey's public accommodation law to the Boy Scouts of America violated that organization's First Amendment right of "expressive association."

Chief Justice Rehnquist concluded that the Boy Scouts had an official position against homosexual *conduct:* It violated the Scout Oath, which says that a scout must be "morally straight" and "clean in word and deed." Because Dale was open and honest about his sexual orientation, Chief Justice Rehnquist decided that Dale's presence as an assistant scoutmaster would send a message that the Boy Scouts accepts homosexual conduct as legitimate and would thereby undermine its official position on homosexual conduct.

Justice John Paul Stevens, joined by Justices Souter, Ginsburg, and Breyer, wrote a dissenting opinion. Justice Stevens pointed out that the definition of "morally straight" and "clean" in the Boy Scout Handbook did not mention anything about homosexuality. Justice Stevens argued that not all the members of the Boy Scouts had the same position on homosexuality. He also pointed out that the Boy Scouts expelled Dale because of his sexual *orientation* (being a gay man), not because of any *conduct* on his part. Justice Stevens concluded that New Jersey's antidiscrimination law did not impose any significant burden on the ability of the Boy Scouts to pursue its goals. Justice Stevens expressed a fear that the majority decision would result in turning "the right to associate into a free pass out of antidiscrimination laws."

In 2003, the Supreme Court revisited the 1986 *Bowers* decision in the case of *Lawrence v. Texas.* As in the *Bowers* case, two gay men, John Lawrence and Tyron Garner, were arrested for having sexual relations in the privacy of a home. They were convicted of violating the Texas sodomy law. Like the Georgia law upheld by the Supreme Court in *Bowers*, the Texas law prohibited certain sexual practices, even in private. However, in contrast to the Georgia law, the Texas law applied only to sexual practices between homosexual couples.

109

In a stunning reversal of the *Bowers* decision only seventeen years after that decision had been rendered, the Supreme Court voted six to three to strike down the Texas sodomy law. For the majority, Justice Kennedy wrote a sweeping affirmation of the constitutional right to privacy, even citing Supreme Court decisions upholding the right of access to contraceptives and abortion. Justice Kennedy wrote:

Liberty presumes an autonomy of self that includes freedom of thought, belief, expression, and certain intimate conduct. . . . [L]iberty gives substantial protection to adult persons in deciding how to conduct their private

Tyron Garner and John Lawrence after a rally in Houston supporting their court victory (June 26, 2003)

lives in matters pertaining to sex.

He quoted from a 1992 abortion rights decision: "At the heart of liberty is the right to define one's own concept of existence, of meaning, of the universe, and of the mystery of human life."

He also resoundingly affirmed the dignity of gay men and lesbians, writing:

The petitioners [the men convicted in Texas] are entitled to respect for their private lives. The State cannot demean their existence or control their destiny by making their private sexual conduct a crime.

In specifically overturning the *Bowers* decision, Justice Kennedy stated, "Its continuance as precedent demeans the lives of homosexual persons. . . . *Bowers* was not correct when it was decided, and it is not correct today."

Justices Stevens, Souter, Ginsburg, and Breyer joined Justice Kennedy's decision. Justice O'Connor stated in a concurring opinion that she believed that the *Bowers* decision, which she had voted for, was a correct decision. Nevertheless, she agreed that the Texas sodomy law was unconstitutional—but for a different reason. She based her vote to strike down the Texas law on the Equal Protection Clause, not on the constitutional right to privacy. Because the Texas law applied only to same-sex sexual relations and not to opposite-sex sexual relations, she concluded that it violated the Equal Protection Clause. She noted that the Texas law branded gay men and lesbians as criminals and subjected them to lifelong stigma. She pointed out that such laws were used to justify discrimination against gay men and lesbians in a variety of contexts, including employment, child custody, and housing.

Chief Justice Rehnquist and Justices Scalia and Thomas dissented from the *Lawrence* decision, arguing that the *Bowers* decision was correctly decided.

The *Lawrence* decision appears likely to usher in a new era of judicial respect and protection for sexual minorities and for the privacy rights of all citizens. David Garrow, a Pulitzer Prize–winning biographer of Martin Luther King Jr., was quoted in *Newsweek* magazine shortly afterward as saying that the *Lawrence* decision "may be one of the two most important opinions of the last one hundred years," as important as *Brown v. Board of Education*.

However, within weeks of the *Lawrence* decision, a proposal to amend the Constitution to prohibit civil recognition of gay and lesbian marriages was introduced in Congress, and by early 2004, President George W. Bush had endorsed the amendment. Marriage, adoption, service in the military, and other civil rights of gay, lesbian, bisexual, and transgendered people will continue to be hot-button issues for the foreseeable future.

"... Nor deny to any Person": Should Students Have the Same Rights as Adults?

The Constitution Says...

"Congress shall make no law respecting an establishment of religion, or prohibiting the free exercise thereof; or abridging the freedom of speech. . . ."
—U.S. Constitution, Amendment I

"The right of the people to be secure in their persons . . . against unreasonable searches and seizures shall not be violated. . . ."
—U.S. Constitution, Amendment IV

"No State shall . . . deprive any person of life, liberty, or property, without due process of law; nor deny to any person within its jurisdiction the equal protection of the laws."
—U.S. Constitution, Amendment XIV, Section 1

Anti–Vietnam War demonstrators at a rally organized by students at the University of California (1965)

For the first century and a half of the country's existence, school policies generally were left to state and local governments and school boards. When the Court finally began to critically examine policies and laws involving students, one of the first issues it tackled was religious freedom. In 1925, it overturned a voter-approved Oregon law requiring students to attend public schools. Oregon voters had approved an initiative to require public schooling for all children between eight and sixteen years of age. The Ku Klux Klan and the Oregon Scottish Rite Masons, who played on anti-immigrant, anti-Catholic, and anti-Bolshevik attitudes to win the vote, had led the campaign for the initiative. The Court unanimously ruled that parents had the religious freedom to send their children to parochial schools.

In 1943, by a six-to-three vote in *West Virginia State Board of Education v. Barnette*, the Court struck down a West Virginia state law that required students to salute the flag each day, even if their religion forbade them to do so. Jehovah's Witnesses had challenged the law because saluting the flag violated their religious beliefs against serving any other gods. The Court's decision was an unexpected one because it came during wartime, when hostility to those who refuse to salute the flag is higher. Jehovah's Witnesses endured assaults, threats to send their children to reformatories, and burning of their meeting places as a result of their beliefs. Moreover, the *Barnette* decision overturned an eight-to-one Supreme Court decision made *only three years before*, in

which the Court had *upheld* a law requiring flag saluting and reciting the Pledge of Allegiance in public schools.

Four years later, the Court voted five to four to uphold the use of taxpayer money to pay the bus fares of students going to school, whether public or parochial. The 1947 decision, *Everson v. Board of Education of Ewing Township*, became a landmark one because, in its decision, the Court spelled out the basic principles underlying the clause of the First Amendment that prohibits the establishment of religion (the Establishment Clause), principles that the Court has continued to follow to this day. Quoting Thomas Jefferson, Justice Hugo Black wrote in his majority opinion that the Establishment Clause was "intended to erect 'a wall of separation between Church and State.'" Justice Black summarized the principles of the Establishment Clause as follows:

Neither a state nor the Federal Government can set up a church. Neither can pass laws which aid one religion, aid all religions, or prefer one religion over another. Neither can force nor influence a person to go to or to remain away from church against his will or force him to profess a belief or disbelief in any religion. No person can be punished for entertaining or professing religious beliefs or disbeliefs, for church attendance or non-attendance. No tax in any amount, large or small, can be levied to support any religious activities or institutions, whatever they may be called, or whatever form they may adopt to teach or practice religion. Neither a state nor the Federal Government can, openly or secretly, participate in the affairs of any religious organizations or groups and vice versa.

These early decisions did not cause much controversy. It was the Supreme Court's decisions in *Engel v. Vitale* (1962) and *Abington School District v. Schempp* (1963) that ignited a firestorm over the role of religion in schools, a debate that has not yet subsided.

The *Engel* case involved a twenty-two-word prayer that the New York Board of Regents had written and that the Union Free School District No. 9 school board, in New Hyde Park, New York, required students to recite daily at the beginning of classes. The prayer was: "Almighty God, we acknowledge our dependence upon Thee, and we beg Thy blessings upon us, our parents, our teachers, and our country." The parents of ten students filed suit, on the grounds that the official prayer violated

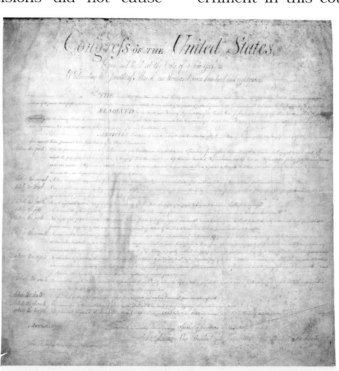

The Bill of Rights (1789)

their and their children's beliefs, and that the prayer violated the Establishment Clause.

The Court ruled six to one that the prayer was unconstitutional. Justice Black, writing for the majority, stated:

It is neither sacrilegious nor antireligious to say that each separate government in this country should stay out of the business of writing or sanctioning official prayers and leave that purely religious function to the people themselves and to those the people choose to look to for religious guidance.

The following year, the Court considered a Pennsylvania law requiring that at least ten verses of the Bible be read daily at each public school. Edward and Sidney Schempp and their children, Roger and Donna, were members of the Unitarian church. They brought suit against the Abington School District. Each morning in the high school, a student from the radio and television workshop selected ten verses of the Bible to read over the intercom system, followed by the Lord's Prayer. Any child was excused from such Bible readings upon a parent's request. The Schempps testified that a number of the selections read were contrary to their religious beliefs, but that they did not want to remove their children from the classroom for fear that this would adversely affect their children's relationships with their teachers and with other students.

The Supreme Court voted eight to one to strike down the Bible reading and prayer, with Justice Tom C. Clark writing the Court's opinion. He ruled that the Establishment Clause means that government cannot give preference to any particular set of religious beliefs, even if the majority of the electorate agrees to give such a preference. He wrote that the Establishment Clause does not prevent schools, however, from having courses in comparative religion or the history of religion. What schools *cannot* do is to promote a particular religion or even religion in general. As Justice Clark explained, the difference between the two clauses is the following: The Free Exercise Clause allows every person to choose his or her own religious beliefs (or nonbeliefs), training, and observances without any government requirements or restrictions. The Establishment Clause prohibits the government from promoting or diminishing any particular religion and requires the government to be neutral with regard to religion.

At that time, there were eighty-three different large religious denominations in the United States, each with more than 50,000 members, and another 18,000 religious groups with fewer than 50,000 members each.

The two decisions caused an explosion of public reaction, with many opposing the decisions. Some who still opposed the 1954 *Brown v. Board of Education* desegregation decision written by Chief Justice Earl Warren used the *Engel* and *Schempp* decisions to renew their calls for Chief Justice Warren's impeachment (even though Chief Justice Warren had not written the Court's opinion in either case).

For the next three decades, with the overwhelming majority of Americans supporting prayer in schools, various proposals to amend the Constitution to overturn the Court's *Engel* and *Schempp* decisions were introduced in Congress. None succeeded.

In 1992, the Court revisited the issue of school-sponsored prayer in *Lee v. Weisman.* The school in that case had decided that there should be an invocation and benediction at the high school graduation ceremonies and had crafted guidelines to ensure that the prayer was "nonsectarian" (that is, not associated with any particular religion or sect). In a five-to-four decision written by Justice Anthony Kennedy, the Court ruled that this violated the Establishment Clause because of the school's involvement in sponsoring and giving guidelines for the prayer.

Although opponents of these decisions often claim that the Court eliminated any type of prayer in schools, some decisions of the Court have allowed religious observance to occur in public schools. For example, in 1990 and again in 2001, the Court ruled that if a school district allows organizations to meet at its schools after hours, then it must also allow religious groups to do the same, as long as the school does not *sponsor* the religious organization. For the Court, the key question in deciding whether the Constitution permits religious activity in a school depends on whether the activity is sponsored by the school or required by law. If so, then this violates the Establishment Clause and is unconstitutional.

Despite the Court's decisions finding that school-sponsored prayer is unconstitutional, a number of schools defy the Court's decisions and have prayer at school functions.

Prayer in schools has been the most contentious issue involving students that the Court has taken up, but certainly not the only controversial one.

Until the 1960s, the Court continued to defer to school district policies outside the realm of religion. As long as a rule was "reasonable," the Court would uphold the rule. That changed with the landmark *Tinker v. Des Moines School District* decision in 1969.

In the mid-1960s, a massive protest movement developed against the Vietnam War. While college campuses were the center of many of the protests, some high school and junior high school students also got involved.

Three students in Des Moines, Iowa—fifteen-year-old John F. Tinker and sixteen-year-old Christopher Eckhardt, who attended two different high schools in Des Moines, and thirteen-year-old Mary Beth Tinker, John's sister and a junior high school student—opposed the Vietnam War. In December 1965, a group of adults and stu-

dents opposed to the war met at the Eckhardt home and decided to publicize their opposition to the war by wearing black armbands during the holiday season and by fasting on December 16 and New Year's Eve. The purpose of the black armbands was to mourn those who had died in the Vietnam War and to support Senator Robert F. Kennedy's suggestion that the truce proposed for Christmas Day, 1965, be extended indefinitely. John, Christopher, and Mary Beth ignored their schools' policy forbidding armbands and suspending any students who wore them. They did not interfere with any of the schools' work or any of the other students. There was no disruption of any classes. Although a few students made hostile remarks to those wearing the armbands, there were no threats and no violence.

John, Christopher, and Mary Beth were suspended until they would come back without their armbands. They did not return to school until after New Year's Day, when their planned protest period had ended.

The students, through their fathers, filed suit, asking the court to issue an order prohibiting the school district from disciplining them for their action. They lost in the district court. The judges on the federal Court of Appeals were evenly split

In 1999, a student, Nick Becker, objected to prayer at his high school graduation in Calvert County, Maryland. Nevertheless, county officials recited the Lord's Prayer during the ceremony. When Nick walked out of the ceremony, the police threatened to arrest him, and he was not allowed to attend the postgraduation party.

Anti-Vietnam War march organized at the University of California, Berkeley (1965)

and did not write an opinion. The students then asked the Supreme Court to hear the case.

In a seven-to-two decision written by Justice Abe Fortas, the Court upheld the students' First Amendment right to protest peacefully. He wrote:

First Amendment rights, applied in light of the special characteristics of the school environment, are available to teachers and students. It is also relevant that the school authorities did not purport to prohibit the wearing of all symbols of political or controversial significance. The record shows that students in some of the schools wore buttons relating to national political campaigns, and some even wore the Iron Cross, traditionally a symbol of Nazism. The order prohibiting the wearing of armbands did not extend to these. Instead, a particular symbol . . . was singled out for prohibition. . . . A student's

rights . . . do not embrace merely the classroom hours. When he is in the cafeteria, or on the playing field, or on the campus during the authorized hours, he may express his opinions, even on controversial subjects like the conflict in Vietnam, if he does so without "materially and substantially

Mary Beth Tinker and her mother, Lorena Tinker (1965)

interfer[ing] with the requirements of appropriate discipline in the operation of the school" and without colliding with the rights of others.

Besides the *Tinker* decision, another consequence of the Vietnam War was the Twenty-sixth Amendment to the Constitution, which granted eighteen-year-olds the right to vote in all elections. Pressure had been mounting for the voting age to be lowered from twenty-one to eighteen because so many young men were dying in Vietnam. It seemed unfair to many that eighteen-year-old males could be drafted for service in a war that could cost them their lives but that they could not vote for or against the government that was sending them to war.

In 1970, Congress passed the Voting Rights Act Amendments, which, among other things, granted eighteen-year-olds (both male and female) the right to vote in both state and federal elections. The Supreme Court ruled in *Oregon v. Mitchell*, a challenge brought to the Voting Rights Act Amendments, that Congress did not have the constitutional authority to extend the vote to eighteen-year-olds for state and local elections but only for federal elections. Congress then quickly approved and sent to the states for ratification the Twenty-sixth Amendment, which grants eighteen-year-olds the constitutional right to vote in all elections. It was ratified in 1971.

The First Amendment rights of students continued to produce controversy. In 1975, three members of the school board of the

Justice Abe Fortas

119

Island Trees Union Free School District in New York attended a meeting of a parents' organization. There they picked up a brochure that listed books that the organization found "objectionable." Ten of these books were in the school libraries, and one was on the reading list for a twelfth-grade literature class. The school board voted to remove nine of the library books and the one from the literature class, calling them "anti-American, anti-Christian, anti-Semitic, and just plain filthy" and saying it was the board's duty to protect the students "from this moral danger as surely as from physical and medical dangers." Of the books removed, one was labeled "un-American" by a school board member because it stated—correctly—that George Washington owned slaves.

Five students filed suit, claiming that

In 1975, the Supreme Court ruled five to four in *Goss v. Lopez* that the Due Process Clause requires that a student facing even a temporary suspension from school must be given notice of the charges, and if he or she denies them, at least an informal hearing. The hearing normally should occur before the suspension, but if the student presents a danger to people or property, or a threat of disruption to the academic process, then within a reasonable time afterward.

they had a First Amendment right to have access to these books at the school. They also said the books had educational value and accused the school board of removing them merely because the books "offended their social, political, and moral tastes." A federal trial-court judge dismissed the students' lawsuit, ruling that the school board had the power to remove books it considered vulgar. The federal appeals court reversed the trial court's decision, and the school board asked the Supreme Court to hear the case.

The Supreme Court ruled five to four in 1982 in *Board of Education v. Pico* that the students' case should not have been dismissed by the trial court, and sent it back for trial. However, the five justices who voted yes could not agree on the reasons for their decision. Justice William J. Brennan Jr., who wrote a "plurality" opinion for himself and three other members of the Court, said that the Constitution does not allow the government to suppress ideas by removing books from school libraries. He quoted from the Court's 1943 decision about saluting the flag: "If there is any fixed star in our constitutional constellation, it is that no official, high or petty, can prescribe what shall be orthodox in politics, nationalism, religion, or other matters of opinion. . . ."

The Court has declined to hear any cases involving the extent to which public schools can control student dress and hairstyle, although it has been asked numerous times to do so. Neither has the Court always ruled in favor of students in First Amendment cases, as the 1988 decision in *Hazelwood School District v. Kuhlmeier* demonstrates.

As part of a journalism course, students in the Hazelwood, Missouri, school district had prepared articles for publication in the school newspaper about the pregnancy experiences of students at the school, and also about how divorce affected the lives of fellow students. The principal ordered faculty advisers to withhold the articles from the paper. He thought the discussion in one article concerning sexual activity and birth control was inappropriate for younger students at the school. He was also concerned that students might be able to figure out the identity of their pregnant peers referred to in the article, even though pseudonyms (fake names) were used. He also worried that the story about divorce included the name of the student, who made various complaints about her parents. (He was not aware that the journalism teacher had planned to delete the student's name from the article.)

The students filed suit, claiming a violation of their First Amendment rights. The district court ruled against them. The court of appeals overturned the district court, based on the *Tinker* decision. The

The books that were censored by the Island Trees school board were:

Slaughterhouse-Five by Kurt Vonnegut
The Naked Ape by Desmond Morris
Down These Mean Streets by Piri Thomas
Best Short Stories by Negro Writers,
        edited by Langston Hughes
Go Ask Alice, anonymous
Laughing Boy by Oliver La Farge
Black Boy by Richard Wright
A Hero Ain't Nothin' but a Sandwich by Alice Childress
Soul on Ice by Eldridge Cleaver
A Reader for Writers, edited by Jerome Archer
The Fixer by Bernard Malamud,
        winner of the Pulitzer Prize

appeals court ruled that the school could not censor the contents of the newspaper because it was a place for students to express their views. It said that censorship was allowed only when necessary to avoid substantial interference with schoolwork, discipline, or the rights of others. The school district asked the Supreme Court to take the case.

A five-to-three decision issued by Justice Byron White upheld the principal's censorship. He ruled that the school had a right to regulate the newspaper "in any reasonable" manner because it was not a "public forum" but was published as part of a journalism course. He said that the *Tinker* black-armband protest was different from the newspaper situation because that was not a school-sponsored activity. He ruled that schools don't violate the First Amendment when they exercise editorial control over the style and content of stu-

dent speech in *school-sponsored* expressive activities if they have legitimate teaching concerns.

The Supreme Court also has allowed schools to invade students' privacy in trying to reduce drug use. In 1989, the Vernonia, Oregon, school district adopted a policy requiring all student athletes (both in grade school and in high school) to agree to random urine tests for drugs before they would be permitted to play on athletic teams. A seventh-grade student, James Acton, was denied permission to play football when he and his parents refused to sign the consent form. They filed suit, claiming that the urine tests were an unreasonable search, in violation of the Fourth Amendment, and that they violated Acton's privacy rights.

The Fourth Amendment to the Constitution prohibits "unreasonable searches" and requires "probable cause" to suspect wrongdoing before a warrant for a search can be issued. The Supreme Court has, however, allowed searches without a warrant when "special needs" make it "impractical" to require a warrant.

In a 1995 decision, *Vernonia School District 47J v. Acton,* the Court upheld the school district's policy six to three. Justice Antonin Scalia, writing for the majority, said that the district's athletes had a "reduced expectation of privacy." They not only had a preseason physical exam (which included a urine test), but they also dressed and undressed in communal locker rooms that had little privacy. Justice Scalia found an important government interest in deterring drug use by school-

Justice Antonin Scalia

children. Justice Sandra Day O'Connor, joined by Justices Stevens and Souter, dissented. She argued that the decision meant that millions of school athletes who have not given school officials any reason to suspect they are using drugs at school are subject to intrusive body searches. She argued that only those students who give the school reason to suspect drug use should be subject to the urine test.

In 2002, by a five-to-four vote, the High Court extended the *Vernonia* decision in *Board of Education v. Earls,* upholding the Tecumseh, Oklahoma, school district's drug-testing policy. The district required all middle school and high school students who wanted to participate in *any* extracurricular activity to consent to urine testing.

At the beginning of the twenty-first century, school policy remains a contentious issue in many school districts. Conflict continues over dress, hairstyles, language, access to books, contraception, teen pregnancy, and abortion, to name only a few areas of debate. We can expect to see continuing Supreme Court involvement in setting the boundaries as to what restrictions schools may, and may not, impose on their students. Since the advent of television in the 1940s and the Internet in the 1990s, it has become increasingly difficult for schools to control the information that students see, read, and publish. The *Tinker* case remains the high-water mark of Supreme Court support for the right of students to express their opinions about matters that concern them.

"Race Unfortunately Still Matters": The Debate over Affirmative Action

The Constitution Says . . .
"No State shall . . . deny to any person within its jurisdiction the equal protection of the laws."
—U.S. Constitution, Amendment XIV, Section 1

Students holding signs outside U.S. Supreme Court after a ruling on affirmative action cases (2003)

One of the most controversial issues in America today is affirmative action. Such policies are designed to increase the number of racial and ethnic minorities or women in colleges, in employment, and among government contractors.

There are many types of affirmative action. These include:

- Actively reaching out to minorities or women by letting them know about job opportunities
- Establishing training programs for women or minorities who are underrepresented in certain jobs
- Setting goals to increase the number of minorities or women at a job site or college
- Providing mentors to minority or female employees or students
- Giving preferences to female or minority candidates who are qualified but whose group is underrepresented

One example of affirmative action is a policy recommended by the Association of American Medical Colleges in the early 1970s. In 1970, only 2.2 percent of doctors in the United States were black, although blacks constituted 12 percent of the population. The ratios of Native American and Mexican American doctors were even lower. In the South, some states had only one black doctor for every 15,000 to 20,000 blacks. Nationally, there was one white doctor for every 599 whites. The association recommended that medical schools admit more students from underrepresented geographic areas and economic and ethnic backgrounds. It set a goal of 12 percent first-year black medical-school students by the 1975 school year. In response, over one hundred medical schools set up affirmative action programs. By 1977, 8.2 percent of the students in medical schools were minorities. In 1978, however, in the *University of California Regents v. Bakke* case, the Supreme Court struck down a special admissions program at the medical school at the University of California at Davis, which allotted 16 percent of its medical-school slots for applicants from economically and educationally disadvantaged backgrounds. The Court struck down this quota system, but the majority of the justices said it was appropriate to use race as one of several factors in deciding admissions.

Showing preference to one group over another has been the most controversial type of affirmative action. Critics of affirmative action argue that preferences are a form of reverse discrimination. They argue that the goal of various civil rights movements has been to create a society where the best qualified person is hired, promoted, or admitted to a school. They argue that society should be color-blind when it comes to employment and higher education.

Supporters of affirmative action argue that preferences have existed for decades. They point out that before passage of civil rights laws, employers could hire and promote white males, openly and legally, over more qualified women and minorities, and that this legacy of prejudice and discrimination still affects the opportunities of women and minorities today.

They also argue that employers have long given special consideration—preferences—to relatives or friends. Many colleges have given admission preferences to children of alumni and/or those who have made substantial contributions, to children of celebrities, to athletes, and to the socially well connected, as well as to applicants from certain geographic areas.

Federal law and many state laws give preferences to veterans (and sometimes their spouses) in civil-service hiring. For example, the Veterans Preference Act of 1944 gives an explicit advantage to veterans and their wives or widows by adding points to their scores on the civil-service test. The Supreme Court has ruled that such veterans' preferences do not violate the Equal Protection or Due Process clauses of the Constitution.

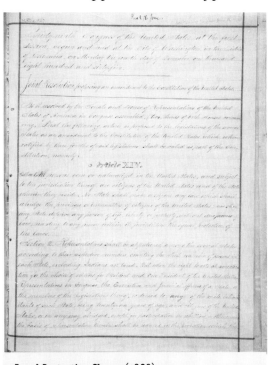

Equal Protection Clause (1868)

The 1990 Americans with Disabilities Act (ADA) involves a type of affirmative action for disabled people. The act does not merely prohibit discrimination based on disability. It requires employers to make reasonable accommodations in the workplace to meet the special needs of people with disabilities.

In some situations, then, affirmative action has been accepted, yet it continues to cause hot debates when it is based on race, ethnic origin, or sex. The debates are particularly intense whenever the number of qualified candidates far exceeds the number of positions available.

To understand how a college or university might use affirmative action, let's consider a hypothetical college in a large eastern city whose student body is predominantly white and from the East Coast. Let's assume it has three applicants, all of whom are qualified, but it can admit only one of them.

John: White, from an upper-class background in New York, attended a small private high school where virtually all of the students go to college. He plays concert piano and won a statewide competition. His grade point average (GPA) was 90.3, and he scored 1275 on his SATs. He has good references.

James: Black, from a middle-class background in New Jersey, attended a good large public high school, where he was class president. He also tutored young students in reading as a volunteer at the YMCA. His GPA was 94.5 and he scored 1200 on his SATs. He has very good references.

David: White, from a poor family in rural Kentucky, attended a small public high school that had a number of deficiencies. During his last two years in high school, he worked thirty hours a week at a fast food restaurant to save money for college. He is the first person from his family to try to go to college. His GPA was 93.5, and he scored 1150 on his SATs. He has excellent references.

Which one of these three qualified candidates should the college admit? Should it be John, whose SAT score is higher than the other two, and whose 90.3 GPA from a top-notch high school is probably "worth" more than the 94.5 GPA and 93.5 GPA of James and David, who did not attend an exclusive prep school? Should it be James, who will bring racial diversity to the white college, and who has shown leadership qualities and an interest in helping others achieve in school? Should it be David, who will bring geographic diversity to the college, has done well in school despite working thirty hours a week, and will be the first in his family to go to college? What if John, James, or David were a female who planned to major in physics, a department at the college that has few female students? What if John, James, or David were Latino or Native American?

Due to the way in which the Supreme Court interprets the Equal Protection Clause, a white candidate who is denied admission has virtually no chance of winning a lawsuit that challenges the admission of white applicants who have lower GPAs and test scores. With few exceptions, the Court allows state institutions to treat people unequally as long as there is a "rational basis" for the unequal treatment.

The Court, however, looks very closely at any use of race or ethnic origin by the government. It does not allow state institutions to consider a person's race or ethnic background unless there is a "compelling" reason to consider race. Moreover, the method that state institutions use when considering race or ethnic origin must be closely tied to the reason race is being used so that there is little possibility that racial prejudice or stereotype is the basis of the government's decisions.

Because of this interpretation of the Equal Protection Clause, white candidates denied admission at public universities have challenged preferences based on race or ethnic origin, but not preferences benefiting other whites that are based on an underrepresented area, being related to an alumnus of the school, or being the child of an important politician or wealthy contributor to the university.

Like the public at large, the Supreme Court has been split on the subject of affirmative action for minorities and women, making numerous decisions over the past quarter century. In 2003, the Court issued two decisions on the same day regarding the use of race and ethnic origin by a state university, the University of Michigan. The two decisions set out the legal principles that now govern the use of affirmative action at colleges and universities.

One case involved the affirmative action program at Michigan's law school (*Grutter v. Bollinger*), and the other at the undergraduate College of Literature, Science, and the Arts (LSA) *(Gratz v. Bollinger)*. Both of the affirmative action programs were intended to increase the proportion of underrepresented minority students (African Americans, Hispanics, and Native Americans). The idea was to make the student bodies more diverse and to enhance classroom discussion and, therefore, the educational experience of students by having a variety of student perspectives. Both schools admitted only qualified students.

Five justices voted in *Grutter* to uphold the law school's affirmative action program, but six justices voted in *Gratz* to strike down the LSA program. Why the difference? Because the law school and the LSA college used different methods to diversify their student bodies.

The law school sought to enroll a "critical mass" of African American, Hispanic, and Native American students. By a "critical mass," it meant enough from each group so that students would not feel isolated, be stereotyped, or feel like a spokesperson for their race. They also would feel encouraged to participate in the classroom. The law school did not use racial or ethnic background as the predominant factor in making admissions decisions but as one of many factors. In its admissions process, the law school used a holistic approach. It evaluated each application individually, using the following criteria:

- Undergraduate GPA
- The quality of the undergraduate school attended by the applicant
- Areas and difficulty of the classes taken
- Law School Admissions Test (LSAT) score
- Letters of recommendation
- The applicant's personal statement, including an essay describing how the applicant will contribute to the life and diversity of the law school

At times, the law school admitted nonminority applicants who had greater potential to increase diversity than underrepresented minority applicants.

The LSA college, on the other hand, used a complicated point system to rank its applicants. Up to 110 points could be awarded for academic performance, and up to 40 for nonacademic factors, with 150 being the maximum possible points. Anyone with 100 points or more was admitted. An applicant with between 75 and 99 points might get admitted. One with 74 or fewer points usually was rejected, or at least the admission decision was delayed.

While an African American, Hispanic, or Native American applicant received 20 nonacademic points automatically based on his or her ethnicity, there were many other ways in which applicants (white or minority) could accumulate nonacademic points up to the maximum of 40 points. These other ways were:

- Recruited for athletics—20 points
- Attended a predominantly minority or disadvantaged high school—20 points

- Socioeconomically disadvantaged—20 points
- Michigan resident—10 points
- Resident of underrepresented Michigan county—6 points
- Child of alumnus—4 points
- Applicant with significant personal achievement, leadership, or public service—up to 5 points
- Applicant who wrote an outstanding essay—up to 3 points
- Points awarded at provost's discretion (with no criteria given for this)—20 points

In addition, an admissions counsellor could flag an applicant for special consideration by an Admissions Review Committee if the applicant did not have 100 points but had at least 75 to 80 points (depending on whether an out-of-state or in-state resident), and if the counsellor thought he or she had special qualities, such as:

- High class rank
- Unique life experiences, challenges, circumstances, interests, or talents
- Disadvantaged socioeconomic background
- From an underrepresented race or ethnic group
- From an underrepresented geographic area

In its decisions on the two affirmative action programs, the majority of the

An *amicus curiae* ("friend of the court") brief is submitted by an organization (or individual) that is not a party to the lawsuit. The federal and state governments do not need permission to submit an *amicus* brief, but private organizations do. Usually, the brief argues in favor of one side or the other in a lawsuit, but from the particular perspective and expertise of the organization submitting the brief. Such briefs can provide the Court with additional information or insights that have not been argued by the parties to the case.

Supreme Court accepted the law school's and LSA's argument that a diverse student body would result in educational benefits. Not only did the University of Michigan argue that this was important, but so did the American Educational Research Association, a number of large corporations, and high-ranking retired leaders of the U.S. military, all of which filed *amicus* briefs emphasizing the importance of diversity for the increasingly varied workforce and society.

Justice O'Connor wrote the majority opinion in the law school case, joined by Justices Stevens, Souter, Ginsburg, and Breyer. Justice O'Connor wrote:

> Just as growing up in a particular region or having particular professional experiences is likely to affect an individual's views, so too is one's own, unique experience of being a racial minority in a society like our own, in which race unfortunately still matters.

She added later in her opinion:

University of Michigan president Mary Sue Coleman (left), with Barbara Grutter (center), and Jennifer Gratz (right), outside the Supreme Court in Washington, D.C. (April 1, 2003)

By virtue of our Nation's struggle with racial inequality, [underrepresented minority students] are both likely to have experiences of particular importance to the Law School's mission, and less likely to be admitted in meaningful numbers on criteria that ignore those experiences.

While the majority of the justices agreed that the University of Michigan could use affirmative action to achieve diversity, the question was whether the particular affirmative action programs used by the law school and the LSA were acceptable. The Court held that a university could set *goals* for minority admissions (which might or might not be met), as long as these were not fixed *quotas* to ensure a specific number or percent of a particular racial or ethnic group. Moreover, the Court held that race or ethnicity could be considered a plus factor, but only in a flexible manner, so that an applicant's race or ethnicity did not become the key aspect of his or her application. Each applicant, of whatever background, must be evaluated as an individual.

Because the Court found that the law school "engages in a highly individualized, holistic review of each applicant's file" to determine "all the ways an applicant might contribute to a diverse educational environment" without assigning "predetermined diversity 'bonuses' based on race or ethnicity," it upheld the law school's affirmative action procedures.

However, Justice O'Connor emphasized that race could not be considered *indefinitely*, and that the law school either had to set a time to end the use of race or had to review periodically whether use of race was still necessary to achieve diversity. She said she expected that all use of race would end within twenty-five years.

Chief Justice Rehnquist dissented in the law school case, joined by Justices Kennedy, Scalia, and Thomas. He argued that although the law school claimed to have only a *goal* of achieving a "critical mass" of minority students, in practice it "managed its admission program . . . to extend offers of admission to members of selected minority groups in proportion to their statistical representation in the applicant pool."

Justice Thomas, in a separate dissenting opinion joined by Justice Scalia, objected to *any* consideration of race by the law school. He asserted that under the Equal Protection Clause, race could be considered by a government institution or agency only in two circumstances: (a) in matters of national security (citing the *Korematsu* decision discussed in chapter 6), and (b) to remedy past discrimination that was caused by that government entity. He also argued that affirmative action stigmatized all blacks who were admitted (even those who would have been admitted without any consideration of race), writing that "because of this policy all [blacks] are tarred as undeserving."

130

Justice David Souter

When it came to the affirmative action program of the College of Literature, Science, and the Arts, the Court ruled that it was unconstitutional. Chief Justice Rehnquist wrote the Court's opinion, joined by Justices O'Connor, Scalia, Kennedy, and Thomas. (Justice Breyer concurred in the judgment but declined to join Chief Justice Rehnquist's opinion.) The Court ruled that the LSA's point system did not allow for sufficient individualized consideration of each applicant. Chief Justice Rehnquist said that assigning twenty points to underrepresented minority applicants was not "narrowly tailored" to achieve diversity and, instead, made race a decisive factor in the admission decision for almost every qualified minority applicant.

Justice Ginsburg dissented in the LSA case, joined by Justice Souter. She pointed out that large disparities based on race still exist in society. She cited various studies and government statistics in writing the following:

> Unemployment, poverty, and access to health care vary disproportionately by race. Neighborhoods and schools remain racially divided. African-American and Hispanic children are all too often educated in poverty-stricken and underperforming institutions. Adult African-Americans and Hispanics generally earn less than whites with equivalent levels of education. Equally credentialed job applicants receive different receptions depending on their race. Irrational prejudice is still encountered in real estate markets and consumer transactions.

She argued that government discrimination *against* minority groups should not be evaluated in the same manner as government actions designed to *eliminate* discrimination against minority groups. She argued that the purpose of the long struggle for civil rights was to achieve freedom from racial oppression, rather than merely to end racial categories. She considered the LSA affirmative action plan, which made explicit the number of

A court can dismiss a lawsuit if it determines that a plaintiff does not have "standing." "Standing" means that a plaintiff must have the possibility of benefiting from the relief that is requested in the lawsuit. Both of the named plaintiffs in the LSA lawsuit had enrolled in other undergraduate schools after being turned down by LSA, and both had graduated from those schools. Neither of them had applied to transfer to the LSA after enrolling elsewhere. Therefore, an injunction against the LSA would not help them, because they had already graduated from college.

points assigned to various criteria, more candid than an affirmative action policy (such as the law school's) that achieved similar results by camouflaging the degree to which race is a consideration.

Justice Stevens dissented on the basis that the plaintiffs in the LSA case did not have standing to ask for an injunction forbidding LSA to continue to use its admissions program. Therefore, he did not address the question of whether LSA's affirmative action program was valid or not.

The *Grutter* and *Gratz* decisions are not the last word on affirmative action. The Court's decision was limited to state universities and colleges. Moreover, it does not *require* state universities to have an affirmative action program—but if a state university has an affirmative action program, then it must comply with the Court's decisions in these cases. Already there are plans by opponents of affirmative action to try to get measures passed prohibiting any use of race by the government for any reason.

131

EPILOGUE

"To Secure the Blessings of Liberty to ourselves and our Posterity"

The *Contemplation of Justice* statue at the U.S. Supreme Court

The Constitution and its interpretation have changed over the past two hundred years. In the half century since the historic *Brown v. Board of Education* decision, there has been an explosion of Supreme Court decisions. The Court has been called upon, time and again, to interpret the Equal Protection Clause. As civil rights movements have gained strength, Congress has responded with laws protecting women and certain minorities from discrimination. These laws are subject to interpretation by the Court. The Court's recognition of a constitutional right of privacy in the 1960s has resulted in numerous court decisions that attempt to define the boundaries of privacy rights.

Of the various civil and human rights issues discussed in this book, only a few seem to have been resolved definitively. The Thirteenth Amendment abolished slavery, and the Fourteenth Amendment granted citizenship to every person born in the United States, thereby overturning the infamous *Dred Scott* decision. The Fifteenth and Nineteenth Amendments guarantee that race and sex cannot be used to deny any adult the right to vote, and the Twenty-sixth Amendment gave eighteen-year-olds the vote.

Most of the nineteenth-century Supreme Court decisions that annihilated the rights of blacks or women have long since been overturned by the Court or by constitutional amendment. There has not, however, been any repudiation of the nineteenth-century Supreme Court decisions that denied Native Americans sovereignty of their own land. Likewise, the Court has not

repudiated the *Cherokee Nation* decision that relegated Indians to the status of "wards" of the U.S. government. Even when treaty rights seemed clear, and even when the Supreme Court sided with the Indians, again and again native peoples lost their land to the ever westward-moving white population.

In one notable case, *United States v. Sioux Nation,* the Lakota (Sioux) Nation pursued lawsuits over their loss of the Black Hills of North Dakota for almost sixty years in the court of claims, the Indian Claims Commission, and the U.S. Supreme Court. Finally, in 1980, the Supreme Court upheld a court of claims decision that the government must pay the Lakota Nation $17.1 million for the land taken from them in 1877 without any payment. The Fort Laramie Treaty of 1868 had provided that the Great Sioux Reservation, including the Black Hills, would be set apart for the "absolute and undisturbed use and occupation" of the Sioux. Only if three-fourths of all the adult men in the Sioux tribe agreed to sell the land to the United States could the land be sold. The United States violated that treaty in 1877 after gold was discovered in the Black Hills, luring waves of white prospectors to the region.

The Supreme Court not only upheld the $17.1 million compensation award, but also upheld an award of interest at 5 percent per year since 1877 on the award. The interest that has accrued on the award is now over $500 million. However, the Lakotas have refused to accept the award and the interest because they insist that the Black Hills should be returned to the

Lakota Nation. The money sits in the U.S. Treasury, continuing to earn interest at 5 percent per year.

Many other civil rights issues also remain in dispute. Even now, new amendments to the Constitution affecting civil rights are being suggested. They range from a new effort by feminists to get the failed Equal Rights Amendment ratified to proposals by antigay organizations to amend the Constitution to prohibit gay and lesbian marriages. Five times during the twentieth century, over half the states passed resolutions, pursuant to Article V of the Constitution, calling for a constitutional convention to propose specific amendments to the Constitution. The concern about such a convention is that it could lead to amendments that might completely restructure our legal system. It could change or eliminate our constitutional guarantees of freedom of speech, equal protection, and citizenship for all who are born in the United States.

Although a constitutional convention is not likely to happen, the founding fathers made sure that it was possible. But it could not be convened easily for frivolous matters or at the whim of a few individuals. If thirty-four states call for a convention, then it *must* be held. Any amendment proposed by the convention would have to be ratified by three-fourths of the states before it would become part of the Constitution.

The Supreme Court will continue to face numerous questions during the twenty-first century. What decisions do you think the Supreme Court will—or should—make regarding some of the following issues?

- Should the Constitution be interpreted to allow separate high schools for boys?

- Should the Equal Protection Clause be interpreted to prohibit discrimination by the states or school districts based on sexual orientation, gender identity, or manner of dress?

- Should the Equal Protection Clause be interpreted to strike down veterans' preferences?

- Should the citizenship clauses and the Equal Protection and Due Process clauses apply to unborn fetuses, or to frozen embryos that are stored for future fertilization?

- Should the Equal Protection Clause be interpreted to require equal per capita funding of all public schools?

- Should Native American tribes be recognized as sovereign nations?

- Should the United States and the individual states be required to honor the terms of treaties made with Indian nations?

- Do state laws that deny marriage to same-sex couples violate the Equal Protection Clause?

- Should the courts allow Congress to restrict some constitutional rights when the United States is at war or under attack?

134

- Should there be affirmative action? If so, what form should it take?

As we explore outer space and probe the inner workings of the human genes, new and different legal questions will need to be addressed by the courts. These decisions will no doubt test Jefferson's assertion that the Constitution "is the ark of our safety," belonging to the living and not the dead. The Supreme Court justices of the future, some of whom are in high school now, will need to remember that the Constitution is a living document, flexible and with built-in safety valves. Yet as important as the Constitution is, it is no stronger than the justices who are entrusted to interpret it and those responsible for enforcing their decisions, from the president of the United States to the classroom teacher, from the governors of the states to the police officers on the street. All of them are spokes in the wheel that rolls toward justice.

WE THE PEOPLE OF THE UNITED STATES, IN ORDER TO FORM A MORE PERFECT UNION, ESTABLISH JUSTICE, INSURE DOMESTIC TRANQUILITY, PROVIDE FOR THE COMMON DEFENSE, PROMOTE THE GENERAL WELFARE, AND SECURE THE BLESSINGS OF LIBERTY TO OURSELVES AND OUR POSTERITY, DO ORDAIN AND ESTABLISH THIS CONSTITUTION FOR THE UNITED STATES OF AMERICA.

ARTICLE I.
SECTION 1

All legislative Powers herein granted shall be vested in a Congress of the United States, which shall consist of a Senate and House of Representatives.

136

SECTION 2

Clause 1: The House of Representatives shall be composed of Members chosen every second Year by the People of the several States, and the Electors in each State shall have the Qualifications requisite for Electors of the most numerous Branch of the State Legislature.

Clause 2: No Person shall be a Representative who shall not have attained to the Age of twenty five Years, and been seven Years a Citizen of the United States, and who shall not, when elected, be an Inhabitant of that State in which he shall be chosen.

Clause 3: Representatives and direct Taxes shall be apportioned among the several States which may be included within this Union, according to their respective Numbers, which shall be determined by adding to the whole Number of free Persons, including those bound to Service for a Term of Years, and excluding Indians not taxed, three fifths of all other Persons. The actual Enumeration shall be made within three

Years after the first Meeting of the Congress of the United States, and within every subsequent Term of ten Years, in such Manner as they shall by Law direct. The Number of Representatives shall not exceed one for every thirty Thousand, but each State shall have at Least one Representative; and until such enumeration shall be made, the State of New Hampshire shall be entitled to chuse three, Massachusetts eight, Rhode-Island and Providence Plantations one, Connecticut five, New-York six, New Jersey four, Pennsylvania eight, Delaware one, Maryland six, Virginia ten, North Carolina five, South Carolina five, and Georgia three.

Clause 4: When vacancies happen in the Representation from any State, the Executive Authority thereof shall issue Writs of Election to fill such Vacancies.

Clause 5: The House of Representatives shall chuse their Speaker and other Officers; and shall have the sole Power of Impeachment.

SECTION 3

Clause 1: The Senate of the United States shall be composed of two Senators from each State, chosen by the Legislature thereof, for six Years; and each Senator shall have one Vote.

Clause 2: Immediately after they shall be assembled in Consequence of the first Election, they shall be divided as equally as may be into three Classes. The Seats of the Senators of the first Class shall be vacated at the Expiration of the second Year, of the second Class at the Expiration of the fourth Year, and of the third Class at the Expiration of the sixth Year, so that one third may be chosen every second Year; and if Vacancies happen by Resignation, or otherwise, during the Recess of the Legislature of any State, the Executive thereof may make temporary Appointments until the next Meeting of the Legislature, which shall then fill such Vacancies.

Clause 3: No Person shall be a Senator who shall not have attained to the Age of thirty Years, and been nine Years a Citizen of the United States, and who shall not, when elected, be an Inhabitant of that State for which he shall be chosen.

Clause 4: The Vice President of the United States shall be President of the Senate, but shall have no Vote, unless they be equally divided.

Clause 5: The Senate shall chuse their other Officers, and also a President pro tempore, in the Absence of the Vice President, or when he shall exercise the Office of President of the United States.

Clause 6: The Senate shall have the sole Power to try all Impeachments. When sitting for that Purpose, they shall be on Oath or Affirmation. When the President of the United States is tried, the Chief Justice shall preside: And no Person shall be convicted without the Concurrence of two thirds of the Members present.

Clause 7: Judgment in Cases of Impeachment shall not extend further than to removal from Office, and disqualification to hold and enjoy any Office of honor, Trust or Profit under the United States: but the Party convicted shall nevertheless be liable and subject to Indictment, Trial, Judgment and Punishment, according to Law.

SECTION 4

Clause 1: The Times, Places and Manner of

holding Elections for Senators and Representatives, shall be prescribed in each State by the Legislature thereof; but the Congress may at any time by Law make or alter such Regulations, except as to the Places of chusing Senators.

Clause 2: The Congress shall assemble at least once in every Year, and such Meeting shall be on the first Monday in December, unless they shall by Law appoint a different Day.

SECTION 5

Clause 1: Each House shall be the Judge of the Elections, Returns and Qualifications of its own Members, and a Majority of each shall constitute a Quorum to do Business; but a smaller Number may adjourn from day to day, and may be authorized to compel the Attendance of absent Members, in such Manner, and under such Penalties as each House may provide.

Clause 2: Each House may determine the Rules of its Proceedings, punish its Members for disorderly Behaviour, and, with the Concurrence of two thirds, expel a Member.

Clause 3: Each House shall keep a Journal of its Proceedings, and from time to time publish the same, excepting such Parts as may in their Judgment require Secrecy; and the Yeas and Nays of the Members of either House on any question shall, at the Desire of one fifth of those Present, be entered on the Journal.

Clause 4: Neither House, during the Session of Congress, shall, without the Consent of the other, adjourn for more than three days, nor to any other Place than that in which the two Houses shall be sitting.

SECTION 6

Clause 1: The Senators and Representatives shall receive a Compensation for their Services, to be ascertained by Law, and paid out of the Treasury of the United States. They shall in all Cases, except Treason, Felony and Breach of the Peace, be privileged from Arrest during their Attendance at the Session of their respective

Houses, and in going to and returning from the same; and for any Speech or Debate in either House, they shall not be questioned in any other Place.

Clause 2: No Senator or Representative shall, during the Time for which he was elected, be appointed to any civil Office under the Authority of the United States, which shall have been created, or the Emoluments whereof shall have been encreased during such time; and no Person holding any Office under the United States, shall be a Member of either House during his Continuance in Office.

SECTION 7

Clause 1: All Bills for raising Revenue shall originate in the House of Representatives; but the Senate may propose or concur with Amendments as on other Bills.

Clause 2: Every Bill which shall have passed the House of Representatives and the Senate, shall, before it become a Law, be presented to the President of the United States; If he approve he shall sign it, but if not he shall return it, with his Objections to that House in which it shall have originated, who shall enter the Objections at large on their Journal, and proceed to reconsider it. If after such Reconsideration two thirds of that House shall agree to pass the Bill, it shall be sent, together with the Objections, to the other House, by which it shall likewise be reconsidered, and if approved by two thirds of that House, it shall become a Law. But in all such Cases the Votes of both Houses shall be determined by yeas and Nays, and the Names of the Persons voting for and against the Bill shall be entered on the Journal of each House respectively. If any Bill shall not be returned by the President within ten Days (Sundays excepted) after it shall have been presented to him, the Same shall be a Law, in like Manner as if he had signed it, unless the Congress by their Adjournment prevent its Return, in which Case it shall not be a Law.

Clause 3: Every Order, Resolution, or Vote to which the Concurrence of the Senate and House of Representatives may be necessary (except on

a question of Adjournment) shall be presented to the President of the United States; and before the Same shall take Effect, shall be approved by him, or being disapproved by him, shall be repassed by two thirds of the Senate and House of Representatives, according to the Rules and Limitations prescribed in the Case of a Bill.

SECTION 8

Clause 1: The Congress shall have Power To lay and collect Taxes, Duties, Imposts and Excises, to pay the Debts and provide for the common Defence and general Welfare of the United States; but all Duties, Imposts and Excises shall be uniform throughout the United States;

Clause 2: To borrow Money on the credit of the United States;

Clause 3: To regulate Commerce with foreign Nations, and among the several States, and with the Indian Tribes;

Clause 4: To establish an uniform Rule of Naturalization, and uniform Laws on the subject of Bankruptcies throughout the United States;

Clause 5: To coin Money, regulate the Value thereof, and of foreign Coin, and fix the Standard of Weights and Measures;

Clause 6: To provide for the Punishment of counterfeiting the Securities and current Coin of the United States;

Clause 7: To establish Post Offices and post Roads;

Clause 8: To promote the Progress of Science and useful Arts, by securing for limited Times to Authors and Inventors the exclusive Right to their respective Writings and Discoveries;

Clause 9: To constitute Tribunals inferior to the supreme Court;

Clause 10: To define and punish Piracies and Felonies committed on the high Seas, and Offences against the Law of Nations;

Clause 11: To declare War, grant Letters of Marque and Reprisal, and make Rules concerning Captures on Land and Water;

Clause 12: To raise and support Armies, but no Appropriation of Money to that Use shall be for a longer Term than two Years;

Clause 13: To provide and maintain a Navy;

Clause 14: To make Rules for the Government and Regulation of the land and naval Forces;

Clause 15: To provide for calling forth the Militia to execute the Laws of the Union, suppress Insurrections and repel Invasions;

Clause 16: To provide for organizing, arming, and disciplining, the Militia, and for governing such Part of them as may be employed in the Service of the United States, reserving to the States respectively, the Appointment of the Officers, and the Authority of training the Militia according to the discipline prescribed by Congress;

Clause 17: To exercise exclusive Legislation in all Cases whatsoever, over such District (not exceeding ten Miles square) as may, by Cession of particular States, and the Acceptance of Congress, become the Seat of the Government of the United States, and to exercise like Authority over all Places purchased by the Consent of the Legislature of the State in which the Same shall be, for the Erection of Forts, Magazines, Arsenals, dock-Yards, and other needful Buildings;—And

Clause 18: To make all Laws which shall be necessary and proper for carrying into Execution the foregoing Powers, and all other Powers vested by this Constitution in the Government of the United States, or in any Department or Officer thereof.

SECTION 9

Clause 1: The Migration or Importation of such Persons as any of the States now existing shall think proper to admit, shall not be prohibited by the Congress prior to the Year one thousand eight hundred and eight, but a Tax or duty may be imposed on such Importation, not exceeding ten dollars for each Person.

Clause 2: The Privilege of the Writ of Habeas Corpus shall not be suspended, unless when in Cases of Rebellion or Invasion the public Safety may require it.

Clause 3: No Bill of Attainder or ex post facto Law shall be passed.

Clause 4: No Capitation, or other direct, Tax shall be laid, unless in Proportion to the Census or Enumeration herein before directed to be taken.

Clause 5: No Tax or Duty shall be laid on Articles exported from any State.

Clause 6: No Preference shall be given by any Regulation of Commerce or Revenue to the Ports of one State over those of another: nor shall Vessels bound to, or from, one State, be obliged to enter, clear, or pay Duties in another.

Clause 7: No Money shall be drawn from the Treasury, but in Consequence of Appropriations made by Law; and a regular Statement and Account of the Receipts and Expenditures of all public Money shall be published from time to time.

Clause 8: No Title of Nobility shall be granted by the United States: And no Person holding any Office of Profit or Trust under them, shall, without the Consent of the Congress, accept of any present, Emolument, Office, or Title, of any kind whatever, from any King, Prince, or foreign State.

SECTION 10

Clause 1: No State shall enter into any Treaty, Alliance, or Confederation; grant Letters of Marque and Reprisal; coin Money; emit Bills of Credit; make any Thing but gold and silver Coin a Tender in Payment of Debts; pass any Bill of Attainder, ex post facto Law, or Law impairing the Obligation of Contracts, or grant any Title of Nobility.

Clause 2: No State shall, without the Consent of the Congress, lay any Imposts or Duties on Imports or Exports, except what may be absolutely necessary for executing it's inspection Laws: and the net Produce of all Duties and Imposts, laid by any State on Imports or Exports, shall be for the Use of the Treasury of the United States; and all such Laws shall be subject to the Revision and Controul of the Congress.

Clause 3: No State shall, without the Consent of Congress, lay any Duty of Tonnage, keep Troops, or Ships of War in time of Peace, enter into any Agreement or Compact with another State, or with a foreign Power, or engage in War, unless actually invaded, or in such imminent Danger as will not admit of delay.

ARTICLE II.
SECTION 1

Clause 1: The executive Power shall be vested in a President of the United States of America. He shall hold his Office during the Term of four Years, and, together with the Vice President, chosen for the same Term, be elected, as follows

140

Clause 2: Each State shall appoint, in such Manner as the Legislature thereof may direct, a Number of Electors, equal to the whole Number of Senators and Representatives to which the State may be entitled in the Congress: but no Senator or Representative, or Person holding an Office of Trust or Profit under the United States, shall be appointed an Elector.

Clause 3: The Electors shall meet in their respective States, and vote by Ballot for two Persons, of whom one at least shall not be an Inhabitant of the same State with themselves. And they shall make a List of all the Persons voted for, and of the Number of Votes for each; which List they shall sign and certify, and transmit sealed to the Seat of the Government of the United States, directed to the President of the Senate. The President of the Senate shall, in the Presence of the Senate and House of Representatives, open all the Certificates, and the Votes shall then be counted. The Person having the greatest Number of Votes shall be the

President, if such Number be a Majority of the whole Number of Electors appointed; and if there be more than one who have such Majority, and have an equal Number of Votes, then the House of Representatives shall immediately chuse by Ballot one of them for President; and if no Person have a Majority, then from the five highest on the List the said House shall in like Manner chuse the President. But in chusing the President, the Votes shall be taken by States, the Representation from each State having one Vote; A quorum for this Purpose shall consist of a Member or Members from two thirds of the States, and a Majority of all the States shall be necessary to a Choice. In every Case, after the Choice of the President, the Person having the greatest Number of Votes of the Electors shall be the Vice President. But if there should remain two or more who have equal Votes, the Senate shall chuse from them by Ballot the Vice President.

Clause 4: The Congress may determine the Time of chusing the Electors, and the Day on which they shall give their Votes; which Day shall be the same throughout the United States.

Clause 5: No Person except a natural born Citizen, or a Citizen of the United States, at the time of the Adoption of this Constitution, shall be eligible to the Office of President; neither shall any Person be eligible to that Office who shall not have attained to the Age of thirty five Years, and been fourteen Years a Resident within the United States.

Clause 6: In Case of the Removal of the President from Office, or of his Death, Resignation, or Inability to discharge the Powers and Duties of the said Office, the Same shall devolve on the Vice President, and the Congress may by Law provide for the Case of Removal, Death, Resignation or Inability, both of the President and Vice President, declaring what Officer shall then act as President, and such Officer shall act accordingly, until the Disability be removed, or a President shall be elected.

Clause 7: The President shall, at stated Times, receive for his Services, a Compensation, which shall neither be encreased nor diminished during the Period for which he shall have been elected, and he shall not receive within that Period any other Emolument from the United States, or any of them.

Clause 8: Before he enter on the Execution of his Office, he shall take the following Oath or Affirmation:—"I do solemnly swear (or affirm) that I will faithfully execute the Office of President of the United States, and will to the best of my Ability, preserve, protect and defend the Constitution of the United States."

SECTION 2

Clause 1: The President shall be Commander in Chief of the Army and Navy of the United States, and of the Militia of the several States, when called into the actual Service of the United States; he may require the Opinion, in writing, of the principal Officer in each of the executive Departments, upon any Subject relating to the Duties of their respective Offices, and he shall have Power to grant Reprieves and Pardons for Offences against the United States, except in Cases of Impeachment.

Clause 2: He shall have Power, by and with the Advice and Consent of the Senate, to make Treaties, provided two thirds of the Senators present concur; and he shall nominate, and by and with the Advice and Consent of the Senate, shall appoint Ambassadors, other public Ministers and Consuls, Judges of the supreme Court, and all other Officers of the United States, whose Appointments are not herein otherwise provided for, and which shall be established by Law: but the Congress may by Law vest the Appointment of such inferior Officers, as they think proper, in the President alone, in the Courts of Law, or in the Heads of Departments.

Clause 3: The President shall have Power to fill up all Vacancies that may happen during the Recess of the Senate, by granting Commissions which shall expire at the End of their next Session.

SECTION 3

He shall from time to time give to the Congress Information of the State of the Union, and recommend to their Consideration such Measures as he shall judge necessary and expedient; he may, on extraordinary Occasions, convene both Houses, or either of them, and in Case of Disagreement between them, with Respect to the Time of Adjournment, he may adjourn them to such Time as he shall think proper; he shall receive Ambassadors and other public Ministers; he shall take Care that the Laws be faithfully executed, and shall Commission all the Officers of the United States.

SECTION 4

The President, Vice President and all civil Officers of the United States, shall be removed from Office on Impeachment for, and Conviction of, Treason, Bribery, or other high Crimes and Misdemeanors.

ARTICLE III.
SECTION 1

The judicial Power of the United States, shall be vested in one supreme Court, and in such inferior Courts as the Congress may from time to time ordain and establish. The Judges, both of the supreme and inferior Courts, shall hold their Offices during good Behaviour, and shall, at stated Times, receive for their Services, a Compensation, which shall not be diminished during their Continuance in Office.

SECTION 2

Clause 1: The judicial Power shall extend to all Cases, in Law and Equity, arising under this Constitution, the Laws of the United States, and Treaties made, or which shall be made, under their Authority;—to all Cases affecting Ambassadors, other public Ministers and Consuls;—to all Cases of admiralty and maritime Jurisdiction;—to Controversies to which the United States shall be a Party;—to Controversies between two or more States;—between a State and Citizens of another State;—between Citizens of different States;—between Citizens of the same State claiming Lands under Grants of different States, and between a State, or the Citizens thereof, and foreign States, Citizens or Subjects.

Clause 2: In all Cases affecting Ambassadors, other public Ministers and Consuls, and those in which a State shall be Party, the supreme Court shall have original Jurisdiction. In all the other Cases before mentioned, the supreme Court shall have appellate Jurisdiction, both as to Law and Fact, with such Exceptions, and under such Regulations as the Congress shall make.

Clause 3: The Trial of all Crimes, except in Cases of Impeachment, shall be by Jury; and such Trial shall be held in the State where the said Crimes shall have been committed; but when not committed within any State, the Trial shall be at such Place or Places as the Congress may by Law have directed.

SECTION 3

142 Clause 1: Treason against the United States, shall consist only in levying War against them, or in adhering to their Enemies, giving them Aid and Comfort. No Person shall be convicted of Treason unless on the Testimony of two Witnesses to the same overt Act, or on Confession in open Court.

Clause 2: The Congress shall have Power to declare the Punishment of Treason, but no Attainder of Treason shall work Corruption of Blood, or Forfeiture except during the Life of the Person attainted.

ARTICLE IV.
SECTION 1

Full Faith and Credit shall be given in each State to the public Acts, Records, and judicial Proceedings of every other State. And the Congress may by general Laws prescribe the Manner in which such Acts, Records and Proceedings shall be proved, and the Effect thereof.

SECTION 2

Clause 1: The Citizens of each State shall be entitled to all Privileges and Immunities of Citizens in the several States.

Clause 2: A Person charged in any State with Treason, Felony, or other Crime, who shall flee from Justice, and be found in another State, shall on Demand of the executive Authority of the State from which he fled, be delivered up, to be removed to the State having Jurisdiction of the Crime.

Clause 3: No Person held to Service or Labour in one State, under the Laws thereof, escaping into another, shall, in Consequence of any Law or Regulation therein, be discharged from such Service or Labour, but shall be delivered up on Claim of the Party to whom such Service or Labour may be due.

SECTION 3

Clause 1: New States may be admitted by the Congress into this Union; but no new State shall be formed or erected within the Jurisdiction of any other State; nor any State be formed by the Junction of two or more States, or Parts of States, without the Consent of the Legislatures of the States concerned as well as of the Congress.

Clause 2: The Congress shall have Power to dispose of and make all needful Rules and Regulations respecting the Territory or other Property belonging to the United States; and nothing in this Constitution shall be so construed as to Prejudice any Claims of the United States, or of any particular State.

SECTION 4

The United States shall guarantee to every State in this Union a Republican Form of Government, and shall protect each of them against Invasion; and on Application of the Legislature, or of the Executive (when the Legislature cannot be convened) against domestic Violence.

Article V.

The Congress, whenever two thirds of both Houses shall deem it necessary, shall propose Amendments to this Constitution, or, on the Application of the Legislatures of two thirds of the several States, shall call a Convention for proposing Amendments, which, in either Case, shall be valid to all Intents and Purposes, as Part of this Constitution, when ratified by the Legislatures of three fourths of the several States, or by Conventions in three fourths thereof, as the one or the other Mode of Ratification may be proposed by the Congress; Provided that no Amendment which may be made prior to the Year One thousand eight hundred and eight shall in any Manner affect the first and fourth Clauses in the Ninth Section of the first Article; and that no State, without its Consent, shall be deprived of its equal Suffrage in the Senate.

Article VI.

Clause 1: All Debts contracted and Engagements entered into, before the Adoption of this Constitution, shall be as valid against the United States under this Constitution, as under the Confederation.

Clause 2: This Constitution, and the Laws of the United States which shall be made in Pursuance thereof; and all Treaties made, or which shall be made, under the Authority of the United States, shall be the supreme Law of the Land; and the Judges in every State shall be bound thereby, any Thing in the Constitution or Laws of any State to the Contrary notwithstanding.

Clause 3: The Senators and Representatives before mentioned, and the Members of the several State Legislatures, and all executive and judicial Officers, both of the United States and of the several States, shall be bound by Oath or Affirmation, to support this Constitution; but no religious Test shall ever be required as a Qualification to any Office or public Trust under the United States.

Article VII.

The Ratification of the Conventions of nine States, shall be sufficient for the Establishment of this Constitution between the States so ratifying the Same.

Done in Convention by the Unanimous Consent of the States present the Seventeenth Day of September in the Year of our Lord one thousand seven hundred and Eighty seven and of the Independence of the United States of America the Twelfth In witness whereof We have hereunto subscribed our Names.

Amendment I

Congress shall make no law respecting an establishment of religion, or prohibiting the free exercise thereof; or abridging the freedom of speech, or of the press; or the right of the people peaceably to assemble, and to petition the Government for a redress of grievances.

Amendment II

A well regulated Militia, being necessary to the security of a free State, the right of the people to keep and bear Arms, shall not be infringed.

Amendment III

No Soldier shall, in time of peace be quartered in any house, without the consent of the Owner, nor in time of war, but in a manner to be prescribed by law.

Amendment IV

The right of the people to be secure in their persons, houses, papers, and effects, against unreasonable searches and seizures, shall not be violated, and no Warrants shall issue, but upon probable cause, supported by Oath or affirmation, and particularly describing the place to be searched, and the persons or things to be seized.

Amendment V

No person shall be held to answer for a capital, or otherwise infamous crime, unless on a presentment or indictment of a Grand Jury, except in cases arising in the land or naval forces, or in the Militia, when in actual service in time of War or public danger; nor shall any person be subject for the same offence to be

143

twice put in jeopardy of life or limb; nor shall be compelled in any criminal case to be a witness against himself, nor be deprived of life, liberty, or property, without due process of law; nor shall private property be taken for public use, without just compensation.

Amendment VI

In all criminal prosecutions, the accused shall enjoy the right to a speedy and public trial, by an impartial jury of the State and district wherein the crime shall have been committed, which district shall have been previously ascertained by law, and to be informed of the nature and cause of the accusation; to be confronted with the witnesses against him; to have compulsory process for obtaining witnesses in his favor, and to have the Assistance of Counsel for his defence.

Amendment VII

In Suits at common law, where the value in controversy shall exceed twenty dollars, the right of trial by jury shall be preserved, and no fact tried by a jury, shall be otherwise re-examined in any Court of the United States, than according to the rules of the common law.

Amendment VIII

Excessive bail shall not be required, nor excessive fines imposed, nor cruel and unusual punishments inflicted.

Amendment IX

The enumeration in the Constitution, of certain rights, shall not be construed to deny or disparage others retained by the people.

Amendment X

The powers not delegated to the United States by the Constitution, nor prohibited by it to the States, are reserved to the States respectively, or to the people.

Amendment XI

The Judicial power of the United States shall not be construed to extend to any suit in law or equity, commenced or prosecuted against one of the United States by Citizens of another State, or by Citizens or Subjects of any Foreign State.

Amendment XII

The Electors shall meet in their respective states and vote by ballot for President and Vice-President, one of whom, at least, shall not be an inhabitant of the same state with themselves; they shall name in their ballots the person voted for as President, and in distinct ballots the person voted for as Vice-President, and they shall make distinct lists of all persons voted for as President, and of all persons voted for as Vice-President, and of the number of votes for each, which lists they shall sign and certify, and transmit sealed to the seat of the government of the United States, directed to the President of the Senate;—The President of the Senate shall, in the presence of the Senate and House of Representatives, open all the certificates and the votes shall then be counted;—The person having the greatest number of votes for President, shall be the President, if such number be a majority of the whole number of Electors appointed; and if no person have such majority, then from the persons having the highest numbers not exceeding three on the list of those voted for as President, the House of Representatives shall choose immediately, by ballot, the President. But in choosing the President, the votes shall be taken by states, the representation from each state having one vote; a quorum for this purpose shall consist of a member or members from two-thirds of the states, and a majority of all the states shall be necessary to a choice. And if the House of Representatives shall not choose a President whenever the right of choice shall devolve upon them, before the fourth day of March next following, then the Vice-President shall act as President, as in case of the death or other constitutional disability of the President— The person having the greatest number of votes as Vice-President, shall be the Vice-President, if such number be a majority of the whole number of Electors appointed, and if no person have a majority, then from the two highest numbers on the list, the Senate shall choose the Vice-President; a quorum for the purpose shall consist of two-thirds of the whole number of Senators, and a majority of the whole number shall be necessary to a choice. But no person constitutionally ineligible to the office of President shall be eligible to that of Vice-President of the United States.

AMENDMENT XIII

Section 1.
Neither slavery nor involuntary servitude, except as a punishment for crime whereof the party shall have been duly convicted, shall exist within the United States, or any place subject to their jurisdiction.

Section 2.
Congress shall have power to enforce this article by appropriate legislation.

AMENDMENT XIV

Section 1.
All persons born or naturalized in the United States, and subject to the jurisdiction thereof, are citizens of the United States and of the State wherein they reside. No State shall make or enforce any law which shall abridge the privileges or immunities of citizens of the United States; nor shall any State deprive any person of life, liberty, or property, without due process of law; nor deny to any person within its jurisdiction the equal protection of the laws.

Section 2.
Representatives shall be apportioned among the several States according to their respective numbers, counting the whole number of persons in each State, excluding Indians not taxed. But when the right to vote at any election for the choice of electors for President and Vice President of the United States, Representatives in Congress, the Executive and Judicial officers of a State, or the members of the Legislature thereof, is denied to any of the male inhabitants of such State, being twenty-one years of age, and citizens of the United States, or in any way abridged, except for participation in rebellion, or other crime, the basis of representation therein shall be reduced in the proportion which the number of such male citizens shall bear to the whole number of male citizens twenty-one years of age in such State.

Section 3.
No person shall be a Senator or Representative in Congress, or elector of President and Vice President, or hold any office, civil or military, under the United States, or under any State, who, having previously taken an oath, as a member of Congress, or as an officer of the United States, or as a member of any State legislature, or as an executive or judicial officer of any State, to support the Constitution of the United States, shall have engaged in insurrection or rebellion against the same, or given aid or comfort to the enemies thereof. But Congress may by a vote of two-thirds of each House, remove such disability.

Section 4.
The validity of the public debt of the United States, authorized by law, including debts incurred for payment of pensions and bounties for services in suppressing insurrection or rebellion, shall not be questioned. But neither the United States nor any State shall assume or pay any debt or obligation incurred in aid of insurrection or rebellion against the United States, or any claim for the loss or emancipation of any slave; but all such debts, obligations and claims shall be held illegal and void.

Section 5.
The Congress shall have power to enforce, by appropriate legislation, the provisions of this article.

AMENDMENT XV

Section 1.
The right of citizens of the United States to vote shall not be denied or abridged by the United States or by any State on account of race, color, or previous condition of servitude.

Section 2.
The Congress shall have power to enforce this article by appropriate legislation.

AMENDMENT XVI

The Congress shall have power to lay and collect taxes on incomes, from whatever source derived, without apportionment among the several States, and without regard to any census or enumeration.

AMENDMENT XVII

The Senate of the United States shall be composed of two Senators from each State, elected by the people thereof, for six years; and each Senator shall have one vote. The electors in each State shall have the qualifications requisite for electors of the most numerous branch of the State legislatures.

When vacancies happen in the representation of any State in the Senate, the executive authority of such State shall issue writs of election to fill such vacancies: *Provided*, That the legislature of any State may empower the executive thereof to make temporary appointments until the people fill the vacancies by election as the legislature may direct.

This amendment shall not be so construed as to affect the election or term of any Senator chosen before it becomes valid as part of the Constitution.

AMENDMENT XVIII

Section 1.
After one year from the ratification of this article the manufacture, sale, or transportation of intoxicating liquors within, the importation thereof into, or the exportation thereof from the United States and all territory subject to the jurisdiction thereof for beverage purposes is hereby prohibited.

Section 2.
The Congress and the several States shall have concurrent power to enforce this article by appropriate legislation.

Section 3.
This article shall be inoperative unless it shall have been ratified as an amendment to the Constitution by the legislatures of the several States, as provided in the Constitution, within seven years from the date of the submission hereof to the States by the Congress.

AMENDMENT XIX

The right of citizens of the United States to vote shall not be denied or abridged by the United States or by any State on account of sex.

Congress shall have power to enforce this article by appropriate legislation.

AMENDMENT XX

Section 1.
The terms of the President and the Vice President shall end at noon on the 20th day of January, and the terms of Senators and Representatives at noon on the 3d day of January, of the years in which such terms would have ended if this article had not been ratified; and the terms of their successors shall then begin.

Section 2.
The Congress shall assemble at least once in every year, and such meeting shall begin at noon on the 3d day of January, unless they shall by law appoint a different day.

Section 3.
If, at the time fixed for the beginning of the term of the President, the President elect shall have died, the Vice President elect shall become President. If a President shall not have been chosen before the time fixed for the beginning of his term, or if the President elect shall have failed to qualify, then the Vice President elect shall act as President until a President shall have qualified; and the Congress may by law provide for the case wherein neither a President elect nor a Vice President elect shall have qualified, declaring who shall then act as President, or the manner in which one who is to act shall be selected, and such person shall act accordingly until a President or Vice President shall have qualified.

Section 4.
The Congress may by law provide for the case of

the death of any of the persons from whom the House of Representatives may choose a President whenever the right of choice shall have devolved upon them, and for the case of the death of any of the persons from whom the Senate may choose a Vice President whenever the right of choice shall have devolved upon them.

Section 5.
Sections 1 and 2 shall take effect on the 15th day of October following the ratification of this article.

Section 6.
This article shall be inoperative unless it shall have been ratified as an amendment to the Constitution by the legislatures of three-fourths of the several States within seven years from the date of its submission.

Amendment XXI

Section 1.
The eighteenth article of amendment to the Constitution of the United States is hereby repealed.

Section 2.
The transportation or importation into any State, Territory, or Possession of the United States for delivery or use therein of intoxicating liquors, in violation of the laws thereof, is hereby prohibited.

Section 3.
This article shall be inoperative unless it shall have been ratified as an amendment to the Constitution by conventions in the several States, as provided in the Constitution, within seven years from the date of the submission hereof to the States by the Congress.

Amendment XXII

Section 1.
No person shall be elected to the office of the President more than twice, and no person who has held the office of President, or acted as President, for more than two years of a term to which some other person was elected President shall be elected to the office of President more than once. But this Article shall not apply to any person holding the office of President when this

Article was proposed by Congress, and shall not prevent any person who may be holding the office of President, or acting as President, during the term within which this Article becomes operative from holding the office of President or acting as President during the remainder of such term.

Section 2.
This article shall be inoperative unless it shall have been ratified as an amendment to the Constitution by the legislatures of three-fourths of the several States within seven years from the date of its submission to the States by the Congress.

Amendment XXIII

Section 1.
The District constituting the seat of Government of the United States shall appoint in such manner as Congress may direct:

A number of electors of President and Vice President equal to the whole number of Senators and Representatives in Congress to which the District would be entitled if it were a State, but in no event more than the least populous State; they shall be in addition to those appointed by the States, but they shall be considered, for the purposes of the election of President and Vice President, to be electors appointed by a State; and they shall meet in the District and perform such duties as provided by the twelfth article of amendment.

Section 2.
The Congress shall have power to enforce this article by appropriate legislation.

Amendment XXIV

Section 1.
The right of citizens of the United States to vote in any primary or other election for President or Vice President, for electors for President or Vice President, or for Senator or Representative in Congress, shall not be denied or abridged by the United States or any State by reason of failure to pay poll tax or other tax.

Section 2.

The Congress shall have power to enforce this article by appropriate legislation.

AMENDMENT XXV

Section 1.

In case of the removal of the President from office or of his death or resignation, the Vice President shall become President.

Section 2.

Whenever there is a vacancy in the office of the Vice President, the President shall nominate a Vice President who shall take office upon confirmation by a majority vote of both Houses of Congress.

Section 3.

Whenever the President transmits to the President pro tempore of the Senate and the Speaker of the House of Representatives his written declaration that he is unable to discharge the powers and duties of his office, and until he transmits to them a written declaration to the contrary, such powers and duties shall be discharged by the Vice President as Acting President.

Section 4.

Whenever the Vice President and a majority of either the principal officers of the executive departments or of such other body as Congress may by law provide, transmit to the President pro tempore of the Senate and the Speaker of the House of Representatives their written declaration that the President is unable to discharge the powers and duties of his office, the Vice President shall immediately assume the powers and duties of the office as Acting President.

Thereafter, when the President transmits to the President pro tempore of the Senate and the Speaker of the House of Representatives his written declaration that no inability exists, he shall resume the powers and duties of his office unless the Vice President and a majority of either the principal officers of the executive department or of such other body as Congress may by law provide, transmit within four days to the President pro tempore of the Senate and the Speaker of the House of Representatives their written declaration that the President is unable to discharge the powers and duties of his office. Thereupon Congress shall decide the issue, assembling within forty-eight hours for that purpose if not in session. If the Congress, within twenty-one days after receipt of the latter written declaration, or, if Congress is not in session, within twenty-one days after Congress is required to assemble, determines by two-thirds vote of both Houses that the President is unable to discharge the powers and duties of his office, the Vice President shall continue to discharge the same as Acting President; otherwise, the President shall resume the powers and duties of his office.

AMENDMENT XXVI

Section 1.

The right of citizens of the United States, who are eighteen years of age or older, to vote shall not be denied or abridged by the United States or by any State on account of age.

Section 2.

The Congress shall have power to enforce this article by appropriate legislation.

AMENDMENT XXVII

No law, varying the compensation for the services of the Senators and Representatives, shall take effect, until an election of representatives shall have intervened.

Spelling, capitalization, and punctuation are as they appear in the original Constitution.

PHOTO PERMISSIONS

FOR FURTHER READING

General

Hudson, David L., Jr. *The Fourteenth Amendment: Equal Protection Under the Law.* Berkeley Heights, CA: Enslow Publishers, 2002.

Irons, Peter. *A People's History of the Supreme Court.* New York: Viking, 1999.

Affirmative Action

Hanmer, Trudy J. *Affirmative Action: Opportunity for All?* Hillside, NJ: Enslow Publishers, 1993.

African Americans

Banfield, Susan. *The Fifteenth Amendment: African-American Men's Right to Vote.* Springfield, NJ: Enslow Publishers, 1998.

Dudley, Mark E. *Brown v. Board of Education (1954: School Desegregation).* New York: Twenty-first Century Books, 1994.

Fleischner, Jennifer. *The Dred Scott Case: Testing the Right to Live Free.* Brookfield, CT: The Millbrook Press, 1997.

Meltzer, Milton. *There Comes a Time: The Struggle for Civil Rights.* New York: Random House, 2001.

Schleichert, Elizabeth. *The Thirteenth Amendment: Ending Slavery.* Springfield, NJ: Enslow Publishers, 1998.

Disability Rights

Nardo, Don. *The Physically Challenged.* New York: Chelsea House Publishers, 1995.

Gay/Lesbian Rights

Andryszewski, Tricia. *Gay Rights.* Brookfield, CT: Twenty-first Century Books, 2000.

Japanese American Internment

Alonso, Karen. *Korematsu v. United States: Japanese-American Internment Camps.* Springfield, NJ: Enslow Publishers, 1998.

Native Americans

Aaseng, Nathan. *Cherokee Nation v. Georgia: The Forced Removal of a People.* San Diego: Lucent Books, 2000.

Students

Nunez, Sandra, and Trish Marx. *And Justice for All: The Legal Rights of Young People.* Brookfield, CT: The Millbrook Press, 1997.

Women

Kendall, Martha E. *Failure Is Impossible!: The History of American Women's Rights.* Minneapolis: Lerner, 2001.

BIBLIOGRAPHY

The primary sources for the book were the U.S. Constitution, the opinions of the U.S. Supreme Court, and the opinions of lower courts. Numerous cases that were not discussed in the book provided background information for the chapters.

Other sources include:

Alley, Robert S. *School Prayer: The Court, the Congress, and the First Amendment.* Amherst, NY: Prometheus Books, 1994.

Aptheker, Herbert. *A Documentary History of the Negro People in the United States,* Volumes 1 and 2. New York: Citadel Press, 1990.

Armor, John C., and Peter Wright. *Manzanar.* New York: Vintage Books, 1988.

Ayres, Alex, ed. *The Wisdom of Martin Luther King, Jr.* New York: Meridan Books, 1993.

Beard, Charles A. *An Economic Interpretation of the Constitution of the United States.* New York: The Free Press, 1965.

Blaustein, Albert P., and Robert L. Zangrando, eds. *Civil Rights and African Americans: A Documentary History.* Evanston, IL: Northwestern University Press, 1968.

Cashman, Sean Dennis. *African-Americans and the Quest for Civil Rights: 1900–1990.* New York: New York University Press, 1991.

Corwin, Edward S. *John Marshall and the Constitution: A Chronicle of the Supreme Court.* Toronto: Glasgow, Brook & Co., 1919.

Cose, Ellis. *A Nation of Strangers: Prejudice, Politics, and the Populating of America.* New York: William Morrow and Co., 1992.

Daniels, Roger. *Prisoners Without Trial: Japanese Americans in World War II.* New York: Hill and Wang, 1993.

Dreyfuss, Joel, and Charles Lawrence III. *The Bakke Case: The Politics of Inequality.* New York: Harcourt Brace Jovanovich, 1979.

Ehrlich, Walter. *They Have No Rights: Dred Scott's Struggle for Freedom.* Westport, CT: Greenwood Press, 1979.

Fehrenbacher, Don E. *The Dred Scott Case: Its Significance in American Law and Politics.* New York: Oxford University Press, 1978.

Flexner, Eleanor. *Century of Struggle: The Woman's Rights Movement in the United States.* Cambridge, MA: Belknap Press of Harvard University Press, 1959.

Foner, Eric. *Politics and Ideology in the Age of the Civil War.* New York: Oxford University Press, 1980.

Foreman, Grant. *Indian Removal: The Emigration of the Five Civilized Tribes of Indians.* Norman: University of Oklahoma Press, 1972.

Freehling, William W. *The Road to Disunion: Secessionists at Bay, 1776–1854.* New York: Oxford University Press, 1990.

Friedman, Jane M. *America's First Woman Lawyer: The Biography of Myra Bradwell.* Buffalo, NY: Prometheus Books, 1993.

Gossett, Thomas F. *Race: The History of an Idea in America.* Dallas: Southern Methodist University Press, 1963.

Gould, Stephen J. "The Hereditarian Theory of IQ: An American Invention," in *The Mismeasure of Man.* New York: W. W. Norton, 1996.

Graham, Hugh Davis. *Civil Rights and the Presidency: Race and Gender in American Politics, 1960–1972,* abridged ed. New York: Oxford University Press, 1992.

Greenberg, Jack. *Crusaders in the Courts: How a Dedicated Band of Lawyers Fought for the Civil Rights Revolution.* New York: Basic Books, 1994.

Hall, Kermit L., ed. *The Oxford Companion to the Supreme Court of the United States.* New York: Oxford University Press, 1992.

Higginbotham, A. Leon, Jr. *Shades of Freedom: Racial Politics and Presumptions of the American Legal Process.* New York: Oxford University Press, 1996.

Horowitz, Morton J. *The Transformation of American Law: 1780–1860.* Cambridge, MA: Harvard University Press, 1977.

Hutchison, Edward P. *Legislative History of American Immigration Policy: 1798–1965.* Philadelphia: University of Pennsylvania Press, 1981.

Irons, Peter. *Justice at War: The Story of the Japanese American Internment Cases.* New York: Oxford University Press, 1983.

Irons, Peter, ed. *May It Please the Court: Courts, Kids, and the Constitution.* New York: The New Press, 2000.

Jahoda, Gloria. *The Trail of Tears: The Story of the American Indian Removals, 1813–1855.* New York: Holt, Rinehart and Winston, 1975.

Konvitz, Milton R. *A Century of Civil Rights.* New York: Columbia University Press, 1961.

Konvitz, Milton R. *Religious Liberty and Conscience: A Constitutional Inquiry.* New York: Viking Press, 1968.

Lawrence, Charles R., III, and Mari J. Matsuda. *We Won't Go Back: Making the Case for Affirmative Action.* Boston: Houghton Mifflin Co., 1997.

Lazare, Daniel. *The Frozen Republic: How the Constitution Is Paralyzing Democracy.* New York: Harcourt Brace & Co., 1996.

Lofgren, Charles A. *The Plessy Case: A Legal-Historical Interpretation.* New York: Oxford University Press, 1987.

Lynd, Staughton. *Class Conflict, Slavery, and the United States Constitution.* Indianapolis: Bobbs-Merrill Co., 1967.

Maltz, Earl M. *Civil Rights, the Constitution, and Congress, 1863–1869.* Lawrence: University Press of Kansas, 1990.

Mathews, Donald G., and Jane Sherron DeHart. *Sex, Gender, and the Politics of ERA: A State and the Nation.* New York: Oxford University Press, 1990.

McKissack, Patricia, and Fredrick McKissack. *The Civil Rights Movement in America from 1865 to the Present.* New York: Children's Press, 1990.

McKissack, Patricia, and Fredrick McKissack. *Taking a Stand Against Racism and Racial Discrimination.* New York: Franklin Watts Co., 1990.

McKissick, Floyd. *Three-Fifths of a Man.* New York: The Macmillan Co., 1969.

Morello, Karen Berger. *The Invisible Bar: The Woman Lawyer in America, 1638 to the Present.* New York: Random House, 1986.

Peters, William. *A More Perfect Union: The Making of the United States Constitution.* New York: Crown, 1987.

Potok, Andrew. *A Matter of Dignity: Changing the World of the Disabled.* New York: Bantam Books, 2002.

Potter, David M. *The Impending Crisis: 1848–1861.* New York: Harper and Row, 1976.

Rakove, Jack N. *Original Meanings: Politics and Ideas in the Making of the Constitution.* New York: Alfred A. Knopf, 1996.

Rogin, Michael Paul. *Fathers and Children: Andrew Jackson and the Subjugation of the American Indian.* New York: Alfred A. Knopf, 1975.

Royce, Charles C. *The Cherokee Nation of Indians.* Reprint.

Washington, D.C., Smithsonian Institution Press Books, 1975; Chicago: Aldine Publishing Co., 1975.

Schimmel, David, and Louis Fischer. *Parents, Schools, and the Law.* Columbia, MD: The National Committee for Citizens in Education, 1987.

Sellers, Charles. *The Market Revolution: Jacksonian America, 1815–1846.* New York: Oxford University Press, 1991.

Shapiro, Joseph P. *No Pity: People with Disabilities Forging a New Civil Rights Movement.* New York: Times Books, 1993.

Sheehan, Bernard W. *Seeds of Extinction: Jeffersonian Philanthropy and the American Indian.* New York: W. W. Norton and Co., 1974.

Skrentny, John David. *The Ironies of Affirmative Action: Politics, Culture, and Justice in America.* Chicago: University of Chicago Press, 1996.

Stampp, Kenneth M. *The Era of Reconstruction: 1865–1877.* New York: Alfred A. Knopf, 1965.

Stampp, Kenneth M. *The Imperiled Union: Essays on the Background of the Civil War.* New York: Oxford University Press, 1980.

Stannard, David E. *American Holocaust: Columbus and the Conquest of the New World.* New York: Oxford University Press, 1992.

Stites, Francis N. *John Marshall: Defender of the Constitution.* Boston: Little, Brown and Company, 1981.

Ten Broek, Jacobus, Edward N. Barnhart, and Floyd W. Matson. *Prejudice, War, and the Constitution.* Berkeley: University of California Press, 1970.

Tribe, Laurence H. *American Constitutional Law,* 2nd ed. Mineola, NY: The Foundation Press, 1988.

Vaid, Urvashi. *Virtual Equality: The Mainstreaming of Gay and Lesbian Liberation.* New York: Anchor Books, 1995.

Washburn, Wilcomb E. *Red Man's Land/White Man's Law: A Study of the Past and Present Status of the American Indian.* New York: Charles Scribner's Sons, 1971.

Weglyn, Michi Nishiura. *Years of Infamy: The Untold Story of America's Concentration Camps.* Seattle: University of Washington Press, 1996.

Wilkins, David E. *American Indian Sovereignty and the U.S. Supreme Court: The Masking of Justice.* Austin: University of Texas Press, 1997.

Woodward, C. Vann. *The Strange Career of Jim Crow,* 3rd revised ed. New York: Oxford University Press, 1974.

INDEX

153

154